Don Whitste

John 14:27

SURPRISED BY THE CALL OF GOD

SURPRISED BY THE CALL OF GOD
Tales of a Jesus Freak

DON WHETSTINE

XULON PRESS

Xulon Press
2301 Lucien Way #415
Maitland, FL 32751
407.339.4217
www.xulonpress.com

Paperback ISBN-13: 978-1-66288-064-3
Ebook ISBN-13: 978-1-66288-065-0

DEDICATION

I dedicate this book to my wife and girlfriend Jenny Sue. You have been by my side since we were teenagers. Thank you for believing in me, even when I had little faith in myself. You followed me across the country, from ministry to ministry, even when it looked like I had crawled out on a limb and sawed it off. As I wrote this book, I became even more aware of how much you mean to me. I can't imagine life or ministry without you. Thank you for co-laboring with me and loving me. I love you dearly.

I also dedicate this book to my son Brent and my daughter Sharianne. You have both grown into very special, caring, gifted people. One of my regrets in life is that when you were growing up, I was gone half the time because of my traveling ministry. I missed a lot of special moments with you. I love you and I am very proud to be your dad.

I also dedicate this book to the many people that God brought into my life at strategic times to model Christ-like living and bump me to the next spiritual level. You know who you are and it was no coincidence that you came into my life when you did. Thank you.

Thank you to Frodo, Sam, and your Hobbit friends. Though you may be fictional, you modeled extreme bravery by underrated people and inspired me to venture into noble quests. And, you modeled the importance of a fellowship.

And, I thank you King Arogorn for your courageous speech at the Gates of Mordor and for modeling great leadership. I would follow you into battle with a pocket knife.

Most of all, I thank you God for counting me worthy to be called a minister and allowing me to co-labor with You in the redemption of the world.

TABLE OF CONTENTS

Introduction xi

It's Here I Trace My Line 1
Growing Up In Franklin Indiana 5
Poor But Enriched By Great Parents 9
Retreating And Exploring 13
Fears Insecurities And The Teenage Years 15
A Preacher Moves To The North End 17
Experiencing The Unexpected 19
Five Foot Two Eyes Of Blue 23
A Second Brush With God 25
Changing Nouns 27
A New Start In A New World 29
Digging Deeper 31
Jenny Sue Is Summoned Home 37
Back Home Again In Indiana 39
Homeless In Joplin Missouri 41
Desiring To Preach 43
Saying I Do 45
A New Ministry 47
Aunt Em And Mrs Stephenson 49
High School Baseball And The Softball League 51
Successful Ministry 53
A Life-Changing Experience 55
Graduation And Departing Missouri 57

My First Fulltime Ministry 59

Life In The Subdivision 61

Growing In Spite Of Obstacles 63

A Divine Appointment At The Wrong Address 65

Our Firstborn 67

Those Who Know, Say Renault 69

Officer Ray 71

Brother By A Different Mother 73

This Is Not Bea Ferrell's Yeast Rolls 75

Moving On 77

Coming Home To A Place I Had Never Lived Before 79

Brown County Ministry 81

Moved By The Jesus Movement 85

New Direction 87

Speaking Of Hippies 89

Seeking A New Wineskin 93

New Beginning In A New Ministry 95

An Eventful Meeting In Whitewater Indiana 99

Thar Ain't None! 101

Jesus Freak Preacher 103

A Brush With Legalism 105

My Own Struggles With Legalism 107

Thrown To The Lions Once Again 109

Where He Guides He Provides 111

A Flurry Of Ministry 113

It's The Church! 115

Vacation Evangelism 117

Delivered 119

Ministering In Haiti 121

Ministering In The Dominican Republic 125

Ministry In The Frozen North 129

ICCH 131

Lovin' Me Some Mexico 133

Living In The Wrong Place 135
Mud, Horse Flies, And Building Woes 139
The Beanblossom Hobby Farm 141
Restless Spirit 143
Loving Ministry In One Place 145
Digging In 147
Small Groups Meeting Big Needs 149
The Door Is Open 151
Teamwork With Staff And Elders 153
New Purpose For An Old Sanctuary 155
Goodbye Home Church 157
Kicked Out Or Called Out 159
Hearing God 161
Camaraderie In Ministry 163
Rescued From The Enemy 165
The Sweetest Witch I Ever Met 169
No Cowboys But Plenty Of Indians 171
A Farm Town And A Plowed Field 173
A Word From God At A Hospital Information Desk 175
Confirmation From A Counselor 177
A Powerful Dream 179
A Download Of Information 181
Under The Oak Tree 183
Lobo 185
Our Garage Church 187
My Spiritual Journey 189
Want To Sit By A Former Bank Robber Or A Former Lesbian . . . 191
Band Of Brothers 193
The J.C. Riders 195
Brad And Deb 199
Tin Man 201
Popcorn And Jody 203
The Boogie 205

Run To The Smokys 207
A Grand Entrance At A Men's Conference 209
Losing Lobo 211
Losing Popcorn 215
Moving New Covenant To Franklin 217
Retirement 219
Losing Tin Man 221
Blessed Retirement 223
Mountain Top High 225
Brown County Sheriff's Department 229
Train, Train, Train 231
24/7 Service 233
Attempting To Minister Peace 235
Jail House Religion 237
Inmate Ministry Routine 239
Racist Biker 243
Role Model 245
The Aryan 247
Is That Like Being Saved? 249
Big Guy 251
Cage Fighter 253
Deputy Don 257
Retiring As Chaplain and Reserve Deputy 259
New Uniform With The Same Department 261
New Priorities 263
Silver Sneakers 265
Music 267

Conclusion 269

INTRODUCTION

It was the end of the summer of 1962 and I had been out of high school a year. I had no goals or future plans, so my life was essentially going nowhere. My job earned enough money to buy gas for my car, cigarettes, and little else. I was struggling with fears and insecurities, I was drinking, Jenny Sue had dumped me, I had drifted from God, and I knew that my life must change. Those concerns may have helped prompt what happened to me on that beautiful summer night, with clouds drifting across the moonlit sky. I parked my car and began walking across the backyard to our house. Suddenly, I felt as if God had taken me in His embrace. I fell to my knees and began to weep. I cried out to God and promised that if He would clean up my life, I would dedicate it to Him and do whatever He asked. When I stood up, I knew that God had called me to the ministry. At that juncture of my life, that was about the most bizarre thing that I could imagine happening to me. Me, a preacher?! I knew, nonetheless, that it was true! After 60 years of ministry, through all the incredible highs and lows of ministry, I have never doubted God's call on my life.

Through the years, some have questioned that I was "called to the ministry". When people asked how I knew that God had called me to the ministry, my answer was simple. I was there!

A few years ago, I was having lunch with a lifelong friend. We have been pretty much joined at the hip since we were twelve years old. Back in the day, we were wild and did a lot of foolish things. My friend looked at me and said, "Whetstine, back when we were running around, I never dreamed that you would become a preacher"! I responded, "Roy, I didn't either"! Yep, this whole called to the ministry thing took me by surprise, but it has led to the most rewarding, fulfilling life that I could have ever imagined living.

This book contains stories that chronicle my life and sixty years of ministry. Many of these stories are pretty incredible, but the credit goes to God, not me. The book is arranged in stories, not chapters, because life doesn't come to us bundled in chapters, it comes in stories. I have purposely tried to avoid grinding any theological axes, just tell my story. I just hope that my story will encourage you to follow your own unique calling and live out your own big story.

IT'S HERE I TRACE MY LINE

"My mom and dad were born here and it's here I
trace my line
To Pioneers who cleared and built their farms
Their presence lingers 'round me as I walk these
hills of Brown
I feel like I am held here in their arms"

My Brown County Home by Don Whetstine
2022 UBP ARR

The words above are lyrics from a song I wrote about my Brown County roots. I was born in Franklin, Indiana, but my family line is traced back to pioneers who first came to Brown County as home-steaders. My mom and dad, both born in Brown County, trace their roots to those pioneers.

My dad, Estal Whetstine, born in 1910 on a family farm on Sprunica Road in Brown County, was the son of Samuel and Nancy Jane Whetstine, who had five sons and a daughter. When I look at the hills and hollows that once were the Whetstine family farm, I wonder how a family of seven people could have possibly made a living there. Well, it wasn't much of a living, meager at best. Dad told me that one cold winter the price of corn was so low it was not worth hauling to the mill. Instead, they picked the corn, put it in the coal bin, and used it to heat their house. During a time when my grandfather Samuel was ill, my dad dropped out of school to run the family farm. He was a sophomore and was never able to finish high school. During hard times, the family could no longer continue on the family farm and moved to Franklin, Indiana. My dad's first job in Franklin was at the Wake-Up Service Station on South Main Street, not far from where the Whetstine family had relocated in Franklin and only a block from where my older sister and I would be born in an apartment where my mom and dad lived after they were married.

My granddaughter, Jazmine, attended Sprunica Elementary School, about a mile east of the old Whetstine family farm. When my dad was Jazmine's age, he attended a one-room school located less than a mile further east from the present location of Sprunica Elementary. I occasionally drove Jazmine to school and told her about the Whetstine family history on Sprunica Road. I marvel that my dad must have walked past the present location of Sprunica Elementary thousands of times, headed to the old one-room school on Sprunica Road. When I was a kid, that one-room school was still standing and my family would stop there while on trips to Brown County to visit relatives. We would often draw water with the hand pump on the well in front of the school. Good memories! When I was a Reserve Deputy with the Brown County Sheriff's Department, I occasionally assisted the Resource Officer at Sprunica Elementary. I find it ironic that my granddaughter attended Sprunica Elementary, where I served as School Cop, about a mile from the place where my dad was born. Jenny Sue and I are very grateful to have lived in our home in Brown County since 1979, raising our kids not far from where both my parents were raised. It is a sweet heritage that I treasure.

My mother, Charlene Margaret Smith, born in Brown County to Thomas and Melissa Smith, lived near Gnawbone. Thomas and Melissa both died about a year apart when my mother was young, so my mother went to live with her older brother Jim and his wife Lucy in Franklin. Mom never talked much about her parents, so I always wondered if those were unpleasant memories. Consequently, I never knew my grandparents on my mother's side and I know little about them. Ironically, when my mother was in the advanced stages of dementia, she began to talk about her mother and tell us that her mother had come by to visit. It gave her great delight to share that with us.

My Uncle Jim Smith loved to play Euchre and often invited people to his home for Euchre parties. My dad responded to one of Uncle Jim's Euchre party invitations and it was there that he met my mom. My mother once told me about that first meeting with dad. She said, "He was kind of short (my dad stood barely above five feet), but I knew that he was the one"! Mom and dad sneaked off to Brownstown to get married, but returned to their individual homes without telling anyone. However, dad's older brother Oren saw the record of my parent's marriage in the Brownstown newspaper and squealed on them. Sometime later, my mom and dad moved into the old apartment house on South Main, where my older sister Judy and I were born. Since there was no hospital in Franklin in those days, doctors came to your home to deliver babies. For six years, my sister Judy was the favored and only child. What a sweet deal she had and then I came along and ruined it! As I grew older, I could never be still, always bouncing off the walls, running my mouth. Much to her consternation, my sister Judy often had to watch me. I was a handful! She made me do girl stuff with her girlfriends. I didn't like it and acted-out pretty badly. It's a wonder my big sister didn't throttle me in my sleep. Today, I am happy to say I have a wonderful relationship with my big sister Judy, my younger brother Barry, and our baby sister Jane. I love them dearly and couldn't imagine life without them.

GROWING UP IN
FRANKLIN INDIANA

When I was one, the family bought a house at 1006 North Hurricane Street in Franklin, across the street from Arvin Industries, a factory that made automobile exhausts. Arvin ran three shifts, so I grew up to the sound of hydraulic presses banging and metal clanging 24/7. For years I found it hard to sleep in a quiet environment. It was when we lived in the house on Hurricane Street, that my brother Barry and my sister Jane were born. Barry is two years younger than I and Jane is four years younger. Franklin was a wonderful place to grow up, especially the north end where we lived. The north end of Franklin was filled with kids close to the same age. We played together every day. The neighborhood constantly buzzed with the sound of kids. We walked to school together, first to Payne Elementary from kindergarten through the fourth grade, then to Franklin High School, for grades fifth through twelfth. It is incredible to think that I graduated high school in 1961 with kids that I first met in Kindergarten at Payne Elementary. Classmates from the class of 1961 still meet monthly for breakfast. That's what lifelong friendships look like.

That's not to say that I was a real fan of school. I was ADHD, with all the accompanying nervousness and anxiety. School, a bit like jail for me, was a long sentence that began in kindergarten and continued through college. It was hard for me to sit still for long periods of time and the creative side of my brain was constantly lit-up with stuff that was much more interesting. I still remember one of my teachers writing on my report card, "Donnie is very bright but he is so nervous". And, yeah, I am still called Donnie by the people who knew me as a kid. I am not sure ADHD was even diagnosed in those days, but I could have been a poster child. My classmates knew I was usually in a parallel universe when I was in class and they took advantage of it. One day a kid poked me and said, "The teacher said that you are supposed to stand and start reading on page 68"! I stood to read, only to see the teacher staring at me in dismay. Everyone laughed but me! Through the years I have come to believe that ADHD is not so much a disorder, as a different way of being wired. Some of the most creative people in the world are ADHD, like authors, song writers, play writers, and stand-up comics. David Letterman is classic ADHD, which is why he is so creative and quick on his feet. If you watch him, you see all the ticks that are common to a person with ADHD. I did like to watch him, because his brain functions like mine.

I liked to read when I was in school, so the school library was my escape. I read books on a myriad of topics. I often had a library book tucked inside my class textbook, reading something of more interest than Biology, Civics, or The House of Seven Gables. I discovered Micky Spillane's Mike Hammer Mysteries when I was in high school and probably read all of them. One day I had a Mike Hammer Mystery tucked in my Civics textbook. Occasionally I would look up to see where the teacher was. Once I looked up and he was nowhere to be seen. Then a voice from behind said, "I'm right behind you Whetstine", and he confiscated my Mike Hammer Mystery.

I excelled in art in high school, because it tapped the creative side of my brain, much like playing the guitar and song writing has in later years. I was offered a scholarship to John Herron Art Institute but, if you wanted to make a living with art in those days, you had to pursue Commercial Art and I liked Fine Art. At that time, my goal was to move to Greenwich Village, where I would paint, write poetry, ride a Harley, and live the Beatnik lifestyle. What a pipe dream!

Poor but Enriched by
Great Parents

I didn't know that I was poor until I started school. When I was in junior high, it really hit me and made me feel insecure. I don't think my parents often had two nickels to rub together. They had grown up poor and passed it forward, but many families were poor in those days, some worse than ours. My parents were hard workers, but my dad's painting and wallpaper business didn't generate a lot of cash. During those days, my mom worked at a laundry, a grocery store, and then the G.C. Murphy Department Store. My dad could do most anything. I remember coming home from school one day to find dad with the floorboard out of his pickup truck, replacing gears in the transmission. I remember wondering how dad knew how to do that. It came from growing up poor on a farm in Brown County. He had to know how to do a lot of stuff.

My dad definitely knew how to hunt and fish and he taught me. I vividly remember a time when my dad took my brother Barry and me to Brown County on a dark night in the spring to gig suckers on the riffles of Salt Creek. My dad had a Coleman lantern with a handle attached to see the fish in the creek and a three-pronged gig to spear the fish. My brother and I walked along the edge of the creek and carried the fish that were gigged. An uncle and my brother-in-law were also part of that trip and my uncle was arrested for gigging a bass. I still remember my uncle gigging what he thought was a sucker and shouting, "That's a damn bass"! Immediately, a voice answered from the dark creek bank, "I'll take that fish"! Unknown to us, DNR Officer Rex Kritser had been following us along the dark creek bank. That was the first time I met Rex Kritser.

Years later, when I was Pastor of the Nashville Christian Church, Rex and his wife Sarah Louise were members of the church. They were great people and a big encouragement to me. Rex would occasionally call and say, "Hey, preacher, what are you doing"? Then he would ask me to patrol with him. I always knew that he needed to talk and I felt honored that he called me. Once when I was patrolling with Rex, I asked about the craziest call he ever received. He said a lady once called to say that she saw a man riding a deer and almost hit him with her car. Rex thought the lady was crazy, but I responded, "No, that lady wasn't crazy, the guy riding the deer was my brother-in-law"! Everett shot a big buck and, when he walked over to gut it, the buck jumped up. Everett grabbed its antlers and ended up riding it across a road where the lady almost hit him with her car. Rex later became our Brown County Sheriff and we remained good friends until he died.

Dad taught me how to hunt rabbits and squirrels. He would carry his Iver Johnson 16 gauge shotgun and allow me to carry his model 67 Winchester .22 rifle. He taught me to look for rabbits in their hutches in the cornfields and weeds. He said, "Look for their eyes"! I have never forgotten that lesson. We often made excursions to Brown County to hunt squirrels on my Uncle Will's property. Dad passed that Winchester rifle on to me when I was twelve. It is still my most treasured firearm and hangs on the wall of our living room.

Mom and dad didn't have a lot of money, but they had a lot of love and wisdom to share. I always knew that my mom and dad loved me and were proud of me. My parents were both very sweet, nice people. My sister Judy recently said that our dad was the most humble person she ever knew. I believe that is true. My mom was a great cook and made the best chicken and homemade noodles that I have ever tasted. At one time, the backyard of the house on North Hurricane Street, had chickens, an apple tree, two cherry trees, raspberry bushes, a grape arbor, and a small vegetable garden. Mom canned fruit and made jelly and juices. She also knew how to wring a chicken's neck, boil off the feathers, cut it up, and fry it to perfection. We ate like royalty on the income of paupers.

I remember walking to Payne Elementary one day with the sole of my shoe taped on to keep it from flapping. Once, when I was on my way to school, my cousin Jimmy pushed me in the creek. I had to skip school that day, because I had nothing else to wear. I often envied the kids with nice clothes and nice bicycles. I remember a kid who had a Cushman Eagle scooter. I really envied him!

I got a job when I was a freshman in high school and worked at odd jobs for neighbors before that, which enabled me to buy nice clothes for school. One of my earliest jobs was at a supermarket. I still remember the boss yelling, "Hey Whetstine, go fight bottles"! There was a huge shed at the back of the supermarket where redeemed pop bottles were piled. Sometimes the pile of bottles almost reached the rafters. "Fighting bottles" meant sorting through that mountain of bottles and organizing them into cartons. I hated to fight bottles!

Later I had jobs at Collins Jewelry Store and Swanks Department Store. I really liked working at Collins Jewelry Store. Collins employed two watch makers and I loved to watch them clean and repair watches.

The magnifying lenses that they wore over their glasses always fascinated me. Mr. Collins was a very kind man and always treated me with respect. He was also generous with Christmas bonuses. One Christmas, he bought me a sport coat that I wore for years. Sometimes, I was sent to the upstairs storeroom to sort and organize things that were sold in the store, or to bring something down for the sales persons. I found the upstairs storage room fascinating, because it was filled with the accumulated treasures of many years of business. When I worked at Swanks Department Store, I often helped in the men's department, sorting men's clothes or helping with sales. I enjoyed that. I wanted to play sports while in high school, but practices were always held after school and I had to go to work.

Retreating and Exploring

I am an introvert by nature, but for most of my life I have functioned like an extrovert, especially during the ministry years. I am also a people person. However, the introvert side of my personality sometimes needs to retreat from people—it's the way I refuel. The outdoors has always been my retreat, my safe place. During my teen years, stresses and insecurities sometimes caused me to retreat. I lived in the last house on North Hurricane Street. To the north were farm fields, woods, wet lands, ditches, and creeks. That's where I retreated. I have always loved studying and observing wildlife. When I was young I had many pets from the wild. My pet raccoon was probably my favorite. I once had nine baby possums, but my mother made me let them go. She didn't think possums were as cute as I did. I often took my Winchester .22 rifle and headed to the woods. Sometimes I shot a rabbit or a squirrel for dinner. I also ran a trap line on Hurricane Creek, trapping mostly muskrats, which I skinned and stretched to sell at a local fur market. I didn't make much money trapping, but I sure had a lot of fun and made great memories. I thrived in the outdoors and still do! That's probably why I love living in the hills, hollows, and forests of Brown County, where the trail head begins at my back door. I often hike through my woods to a connecting trail that runs along Beanblossom Creek. I still love to explore!

My Ford Ranger pickup has a cap that is set-up for camping. I have a sticker on one of the windows that reads "Bigfoot Pursuit Vehicle". I sometimes go to a State Park or State Forest to solo hike and camp. After completing training to become a Reserve Deputy, I felt drained, so I took a solo trip out west to camp, hike, explore, and seek God. A couple of years earlier, I had been in Oregon climbing mountains with Jenny Sue's brother Lee. On my flight home, I had a window seat and marveled at the scenery below. I longed to see that country from ground level and, after completing Deputy training, the timing seemed good. For ten days, I had few long conversations with anyone but God. It was heavenly and I came back rejuvenated and refocused. Sometimes people suggest that I should not camp and hike alone, but "alone" is my goal. It's one of the places where I hear God's voice the clearest.

FEARS INSECURITIES AND THE TEENAGE YEARS

It seemed that all my fears and insecurities surfaced in my teen years. I felt a constant need to prove myself. Then too, my ADHD brain was always scheming-up some sort of mischief. The boys I ran with were often in trouble, so I was too! I remember my mother saying, "If those boys jumped in the fire, you would jump in with them". I think that was pretty accurate. We stole and vandalized, mostly because we were just bored. We also played a game after dark called "bugging the town". We would cause a disturbance so that the police were called, then run away, encouraging the police to chase us. Once we waited for the police to drive down our alley and we threw eggs on the patrol car from the top of a shed. We climbed down from the shed and ran away before the policemen could get out of their patrol car. The police drove down our alley about every night shining their spotlight on our backyard, to see what my brother and I were up to. One Halloween, I sneaked into the patrol cars at the police station and soaped the windows from inside the cars. I was considered legend after that stunt and that was what I wanted, to prove that I was more than just a scrawny poor kid from the north end of Franklin—I had skills!

Many of the families in the north end of Franklin, transplants from Kentucky and Tennessee, moved to Franklin to work at Arvin

Industries. Through the years, people have asked where I got my southern accent. I got it in Franklin, Indiana, from the people I grew up with, which included my brother-in-law Everett, who was from Kentucky and like a big brother to me. Some of the people in Franklin looked down on people from the north end. Before I was born, the downtown Franklin churches started a church in the north end to minister to people like us. Some interpreted that to mean that we were not welcome in the downtown churches—we were considered inferior. Whether or not it was true, I internalized that message. Being a scrawny poor kid only intensified my feelings of inferiority. I began to act inferior. I smoked and drank before I was old enough to buy cigarettes and alcohol. I was not a nice person. Before I finished high school, I had been arrested several times and spent a year on probation. I had great parents. There was no reason for me to be so dysfunctional, except for one big problem. I didn't really know Jesus!

A Preacher Moves to the North End

I do not recall exactly when Don Knoy moved to the north end to minister at Franklin Memorial Church, but he made an immediate impact on our community. He was about the happiest person I ever met. My family began attending church more regularly. My dad, mom, and older sister Judy accepted Christ and were baptized. I remember my sister Judy standing behind the coal stove in the living room trying to warm up after she came home from being baptized in the old concrete baptistry under the stage at Franklin Memorial Church. The water was never very warm. I also noticed that my dad stopped spending as much time at my uncle's house and coming home drunk. I watched him sit for hours on the corner of the couch near a window, reading his Bible. And, Don Knoy began spending a lot of time at our house, talking with mom and dad. I didn't know what to make of that.

After I erected a basketball goal on the back of our garage, half the neighborhood kids were there in the evening, hanging around, or playing basketball in the alley. Don Knoy began to join us. When we saw him coming, we warned our friends to watch their language. One evening, the preacher asked if we would like to go to Christian Service Camp that summer. Christian Service! That did not sound like fun to me! I asked the preacher if there would be girls there and he said yes. That's what convinced me to give this camp thing a try. Several of my friends and I went to that week of camp held at McCormick's Creek State Park. We took a carton of cigarettes and a pint of whiskey. Did I mention that it was a Baptist Camp?!

Experiencing the Unexpected

I didn't know what to expect from the week of camp at McCormick's Creek. I had never been to camp before and it was all new to me. I still remember the cool breeze blowing across the campground in the evening and the sound of teens laughing and talking. The rules for the week of camp were explained shortly after we arrived. We were told to stay out of a sinkhole cave across the road. Naturally, my buddies and I were exploring that cave within the hour. We were also told to stay out of a cave behind the boy's dormitory, because teens in the past had used it to smoke. Yep, that's where we smoked.

In the evening of the first day in camp, a voice over the loud-speaker announced that it was time for Vespers. I didn't even know what Vespers was! Vespers turned out to be the evening worship and preaching service that was held in a beautiful amphitheater. A lady led some worship songs and a tall black man, blind in one eye, began to preach. I had heard preaching before, but not like this man preached. It was riveting and I felt like he was talking straight to me. It was a pure Gospel sermon dealing with the death, burial, and resurrection of Jesus. By the time he finished his sermon, I was absolutely convinced that I needed to accept Jesus as my Savior. I did not do it that night, but I was strongly convicted. I was dealing with feelings that I had never experienced before.

At the second vesper service, I responded to the invitation to accept Jesus as my Savior. I went forward, shaking with emotion and conviction. The preacher asked me to repeat the Good Confession after him, but I could not speak. Nothing would come out of my mouth! Finally, he told me to just nod agreement as he phrased the Good Confession, so I nodded. He prayed for me and several other teens who accepted Christ that night. It was scary and wonderful at the same time. I had never experienced anything like that, it rocked my world! Several of my friends also accepted Christ and, as soon as we got back to the campground, we threw away our cigarettes and booze. On Wednesday night following camp, Don Knoy baptized me and a few others in that old concrete baptistry under the stage at Franklin Memorial Church. Luckily, it was summer, so the water wasn't as cold as when my sister Judy was baptized.

To this day, when I think about that week of camp at McCormick's Creek State Park, the emotions come rushing back. McCormick's Creek is one of my favorite places to solo camp and hike. My time there usually includes sitting in that amphitheater, praying and reflecting on that week of camp where Jesus became real to me. That amphitheater is a sacred place—hallowed ground.

When I returned home from camp, I believed that the only way I could remain a Christian, was to avoid my friends. I feared they might drag me back into my former behavior. I basically hid out until school started. I also attended about every service or function at Franklin Memorial Church. I attended Sunday morning and evening worship services. I went to youth group and midweek Bible study. When I found out about choir practice on Thursday night, I began attending that. I remember walking home from the church one night asking God if he could please prompt the leaders of the church to start a service every night. I think I was probably trying to live the Christian life defensively. It didn't work!

When the summer break was over and school started, I found myself hanging out with the same knuckleheads as before, listening to the same coarse talk, and being around the same bad behavior. Gradually, I began participating in it, but something had changed. I had developed a conscience. I felt guilt and shame practicing the same behavior that I once enjoyed. Sin was no longer fun—it grieved me!

FIVE FOOT TWO EYES OF BLUE

A very good thing happened to me in my teen years. One day, a cute blond walked across the study hall and I took notice. Like the song says, she was five foot two with eyes of blue. Her name was Jenny Sue Ryker and she had transferred to our school the previous year. She was a sophomore and I was a junior. I remember asking her to dance with me at a dance held at the City Building. While we danced, I asked her name and she said it was Jenny Sue. I asked if Jenny was short for Jennifer and she bristled and said, "No, my name is Jenny Sue"!

Eventually, I got up the nerve to ask Jenny Sue if I could walk her home from school. Actually, it wasn't a very nervy move. My brother's locker was next to Jenny Sue's and I asked him to pass her a note asking permission to walk her home. I guess I thought it would be easier to bear the rejection that way, if she said no. She actually said yes and I met her at her locker and walked her to her home on West Madison Street. She was wearing a pink sweater and a green wool skirt. We ate Girl Scout cookies, drank milk, and played a game of Pickup Sticks. Sarah Lee, Jenny Sue's mother, observed something that I did during the game and said, "How noble"! To this day, I don't have a clue what I did that could be considered noble.

Jenny Sue and I dated for the next year or so, but it was an on and off relationship. After I accepted Christ at camp, regardless of my spiritual state, I regularly attended church with my family at Franklin Memorial. While we were dating, Jenny Sue began attending with me. She gave her life to Christ and was baptized. That was great! She graduated high school a year after I did and was offered a scholarship to Franklin College. Since I did not have the GPA or funds to go to college, I had never even considered it. I was the first in my immediate family to graduate high school —college just wasn't on my radar. I figured my career would be working at Arvin Industries. I was hired at Arvin, but they fired me after two weeks for not coming to work one night. After that, I worked as a carpenter with my brother-in-law, but he joined the Carpenters Union, so I had to find another job. I found a job at Western Auto in Franklin. I really enjoyed working at Western Auto, where I sold auto parts, mounted tires, and delivered appliances. Unfortunately, there wasn't much hope for advancement and the salary was meager.

In the summer of 1962, Jenny Sue began making plans to attend Franklin College and decided her future plans would not include me. She had a heart-to-heart with me and shot pretty straight. She said that she didn't see me having much of a future and, if she stayed with me, she wouldn't either. Ouch, that hurt, but it was true!

A Second Brush with God

It was a shot of reality to be dumped by the girl I loved. I did some deep introspection. Yeah, my life was going nowhere and I didn't see a clear path forward. The drinking that I was doing wasn't helping either, just made me depressed. Now, back to the introduction to this book, where I described my emotional and spiritual state on that night in the summer of 1962. Whether or not it was a conscious thing, my soul was seeking God. In response to my need, He embraced me. I fell to my knees, wept bitterly, and promised God that, if He would clean-up my life, I would give it to Him and do whatever He asked. As I said in the introduction of the book, when I got up from my knees, I knew that God had called me to the ministry. But, what did that mean?! How do you become a minister?! I really didn't have a clue, so I decided to ask a minister.

We had a new minister at Franklin Memorial, whose name was Sonny. I went to his house and explained what had happened to me in my backyard a few days before and said that I believed God had called me to the ministry. He agreed and said that I needed to attend Ozark Bible College in Joplin, Missouri. He said the fall semester began in two weeks and, if I would commit to attending, he would make it possible for me to enroll. Sonny then asked the leaders of Franklin Memorial to sponsor me to attend Ozark Bible College, since I was the first young man to commit to the ministry in the church's history. The leaders graciously offered to pay for my tuition and books for as long as I attended Ozark Bible College. And, they did! What a blessing!

After talking to Sonny and the leaders of Franklin Memorial, I went to see Jenny Sue. I told her about my experience in my back-yard and my plan to become a minister. It was not a ploy to get her back. Even though we were no longer dating, she was a friend and I wanted to share my good news. I also shared the same news with some of the guys I ran around with. They laughed and took bets on how long it would last. Ironically, one of them also became a minister. As I talked to Jenny Sue about Ozark Bible College and my plan to become a minister, she decided she would also like to attend OBC. Jenny Sue gave up her scholarship to Franklin College and informed her parents that she was going to OBC. That was not good news to her parents. After she committed to attend OBC, Franklin Memorial paid for Jenny Sue's tuition and books.

I am so thankful for the people at Franklin Memorial, who were so supportive to Jenny Sue and I through the years.

CHANGING MY NOUNS

As a Jail Chaplain, I told the inmates, if they wanted to change, they needed to change their nouns—persons, places, and things. That's exactly what the move to Joplin, Missouri did for me. I totally changed my nouns. I arrived in Joplin a week before school started, because I needed to find a job. Even though Franklin Memorial had covered the cost of tuition and books, I needed money for dorm rent and other necessities. My brother-in-law drove me to Joplin, accompanied by my father and my older sister. Since the college was not in session, the men's dormitory was not open. I talked with Don Earl Boatman, the president of the college, and he opened the dormitory so that I would have a place to stay. I spent my first night in Joplin, alone in the men's dorm. Other than the president of the college, whom I had just met, I did not know one other person in Joplin. It was one of the loneliest nights of my life. Bill Rachel dropped by the dorm the next day. He had also come to Joplin early to find a job before enrolling at OBC. We became instant friends and I was lonely no more.

I found a job at a Smith's Paint Store, which enabled me to pay my living expenses for my freshman year of college. I really enjoyed working at the paint store. I had experience in building and painting, having worked as a carpenter with my brother-in-law and with my dad at his painting and wallpaper business. At Smith's Paint Store, I sold paint, painting equipment, drywall supplies, flooring tile, etc.

Plus, I stocked shelves with all the materials sold in the store. I really hated leaving that job at the close of the school year, when I returned home for the summer.

A New Start in a New World

I did not know what to expect of Bible College, since it was all new to me. As the men's dormitory began to fill with students, I felt like my whole world was expanding. I met students from many states in our nation and from many countries of the world. I really enjoyed the students from South Africa, Australia, Jamaica, and Mexico. Their accents and lifestyles were so different than anything I had experienced in my Indiana small town. I never grew tired of hearing them talk about their home countries. I bonded with several of my dorm mates and we became good buds. I especially enjoyed our evening devotions and prayer times in the dorm. I felt like God had lit a fire in me and it was good!

Soon, Jenny Sue arrived and settled in the women's dorm and it was good to be with her again. We became good friends with many OBC students, as we attended classes together and took part in campus activities. One of our favorite destinations was Duroy's, a restaurant located a few blocks from the old campus on Wall Street, where Jenny Sue and I often hung out together or with friends. Duroy's made great thick milk shakes.

During our first year at OBC, Jenny Sue and I began singing together and discovered that we harmonized well. The first time we sang together was at a revival at a church in Joplin. We have been singing together ever since. The OBC professors often preached at area churches on weekend and invited students to participate, singing or giving testimonies. It was a real treat to be invited to one of those events.

When we began our studies at OBC, the college was located on North Wall Street and the campus was very compact. The Administration Building was a huge mansion that the college had bought and repurposed. There were offices, class rooms, and a bookstore located on the main floor, with a dining hall, more classrooms, and a print shop in the basement. The second floor was the women's dorm. The college built an annex onto the Administration Building, which contained more classrooms and the chapel. A house next to the annex, served as the music hall, where music classes were held. A large two story house across the street from the Administration Building, served as the men's dorm. During our freshman year, there were only a few hundred students at the college and, with most of the professors and administrators living nearby, we knew just about everyone associated with the college. I loved the cozy feeling we experienced on the old North Wall Street campus and I missed that a bit as the college grew and relocated to its new campus on North Main Street.

DIGGING DEEPER

When classes began in the fall of 1962, I found myself immersed in the Bible. I was given a Bible when I was baptized, but it was a King James Version and I found it hard to understand, a bit confusing. One of the first things I did was to buy a version of the Bible that I could understand and began reading it. Between my classes and my own personal reading, I began to grow in my understanding of my role in this world. I felt like God was preparing me for some grand purpose. After sixty years of ministry, I still feel like I have a grand purpose. Three things changed immediately after my brush with God at nineteen, I felt like I had worth, identity, and purpose. That feeling grew as I studied at OBC.

The OBC Professors didn't just teach the Bible, they led the students in following Christ. The motto of the college is: The Word of Christ taught in the Spirit of Christ. Discipleship was never meant to be a rigid, sterile course in doctrine. Biblical discipleship requires relationships. Jesus called his disciples by saying, "Take my yoke upon you". The "yoke" of a Rabbi was two things: his teachings and his lifestyle. When a Rabbi called a potential disciple, he offered to share, not just his teachings, but his life with them. That's what I received from my professors at OBC. As they taught me, they took time for me and cared about me. They also led by example, for they walked with Jesus. Don DeWelt, one of my favorite professors, arose at 4 AM, dressed for his classes, and spent an hour in prayer before he came to the college to teach. I remember passing his house in the wee hours of the morning and seeing the light on in his study. That spoke volumes to me!

I appreciated all my professors at OBC, but Don DeWelt was one of my favorites, because he made the Scriptures come to life. I took Old Testament History, Acts of the Apostles, the Pastoral Epistles, and Homiletics under Brother DeWelt. To this day, I can hear his voice in my head as I read Scriptures that he covered in class. Brother DeWelt challenged his students to memorize the Scriptures as we studied them. I discovered that I had a knack for memorization, because I had a photographic memory. After I intensely studied a passage of Scripture, I could see it in my head. I memorized the letters of First Timothy, Second Timothy, and Titus while taking the Pastoral Epistles under Brother DeWelt. I also memorized many other sections of Scripture. Sometimes, before we studied a portion of the Pastoral Epistles in class, Brother DeWelt would ask me to quote that section of Scripture. During my senior year at OBC, he once asked me to teach the Pastoral Epistles class in his absence, which was a great honor. Brother DeWelt rewarded me for my memorization of Scripture by exempting me from some of the "busy work" assignments in his classes. The memorization of Scripture that I did in college has proven to be a great blessing in my teaching and preaching. Thank you, Brother DeWelt, for encouraging me to memorize Scripture.

I am grateful to have taken Homiletics, the art of preaching, under Brother DeWelt, for he was one of the best preachers I have ever heard. Our textbook for the class was a book that he authored. In fact, all the classes that he taught utilized a textbook that he authored. As in all his classes, he emphasized memorization in Homiletics class. I still remember him saying, "The best place to write down your sermon is on the inside of your skull". That has served me well through the years and, to this day, I have few notes when I preach. My sermon is usually written on the inside of my skull, with a skeleton outline in my Bible. I also remember him saying, "People's minds can only absorb what their posteriors can endure". In other words, don't preach too long. Long sermons are a bit like holding people hostage. Brother DeWelt stressed that the purpose of preaching is to "prove, correct, and encourage", as Paul instructed Timothy. He said that a lot of preachers were "big on proving and correcting, but weak on encouraging". Through the years, I have tried to be mindful of that when I preach. Preaching must encourage the hearer and, in this negative world, the hearers need all the encouragement they can get.

When I met Brother DeWelt in the hallways of OBC and asked how he was, his answer was always the same—"I am happy on my way to Heaven". He is there now and happier than ever.

Another favorite professor was Seth Wilson, the Dean of OBC. Seth was one of the most intelligent men I ever met, a wealth of knowledge. He could tell you how to adjust the valves on your car, mix concrete, or interpret a Greek word. Seth usually wrote on the chalk board as he lectured and his English often, unconsciously, turned to Greek. I remember Seth saying, "excuse my Greek". Then he would erase the Greek words and substitute English words. You could flunk a class taught by Brother Wilson and still learn a lot. Once while studying in the OBC Library, I had a question about something. Seth was in his office nearby, so I asked for his input. He responded by saying that he could not sufficiently answer my question at that location and I needed to follow him to his personal library in his home. I drove to his home and he led me into his private library. I was amazed to find that Seth had more volumes on the subject in his personal library, than were to be found in the OBC Library. He pulled several reference books from the shelves and gave me a very scholarly answer to my question.

I took several classes under Brother Wilson. Two of my favorites were Hermeneutics and Life of Christ. Hermeneutics, the science of interpreting the Scriptures, taught valuable lessons that have guided me through many years of Bible study. I received an A- in Hermeneutics class, which was the best grade Seth gave. He said that an A represented perfection and there is always more to learn.

Life of Christ was another favorite class taught by Brother Wilson. On the first day of class, he gave us a detailed five-page outline of the life of Christ and told us that we had two weeks to memorize it. He then gave us a sixth page, which was a condensed version of the five-page outline. He said that if we memorized the sixth page first, the other five pages would be easier to memorize. I remember a couple of students who looked over the outline and dropped the class that day. Fortunately, my ability to memorize made this assignment doable. I am grateful that I memorized that outline of the life of Christ. As Brother Wilson taught through the life of Christ, I sometimes felt like I was walking along with Jesus. What a blessing to be instructed by this great man of God. I will never forget his teachings or his public prayers. Seth Wilson walked with God.

Professor Wilbur Fields, an unforgettable influence on my life, taught classes on the Old Testament and Archeology. Brother Fields treated all his students equally, he showed no favoritism. All his students were mutually encouraged. He had spent many of his summer breaks on archeological digs in Israel and knew that country like the back of his hand. Wilbur often took students with him on archeological digs. I dreamed of one day accompanying him on one of his digs, but was never able to do that. I will never forget Wilbur opening his Hebrew Bible from the back, since Hebrew is read backwards to English, and translating Hebrew to English as he read. I will also never forget his resounding voice as he lectured or poured encouragement on his students. I feel very privileged to have been instructed by this great man of God.

I was also privileged to be instructed by Bob Stacy. I took several classes from Brother Stacy in the five years that I studied at OBC. I still remember him explaining an Old Testament verse and loudly exclaiming, "Man, that is terse"! Bob was one of the coolest professors at OBC and closest to the age of his students. I liked Bob!

While at OBC, I sang with a couple of different choirs and men's quartets. Bob Stacy asked one of those quartets to become part of a new High School Assembly Team that he was forming. There was also a women's trio and a soloist. The soloist was a young lady from Japan, who dressed in traditional Japanese attire and sang in Japanese. After the musical part of the presentation, Brother Bob preached messages that were very humorous and connected well with the teens. I still remember lines from his sermons. We traveled to numerous schools near Joplin and sometimes took weekend trips to other states.

One weekend trip to Indiana was quite memorable. I had volunteered to drive my car and transport some of the team members, but I discovered the previous day that the water pump on my car was leaking. I was working at Safeway Supermarket at the time and, when I got off work that evening, one of the team members and I replaced the water pump on my '55 Chrysler. It was after five PM when we started our project, so we had to ask a man to reopen his parts store to buy a new water pump. Jenny Sue and I were married at the time, so my friend and I worked all night on the curb in front of our apartment to replace that water pump and finished just as the sun was coming up. We packed our bags in the car, met the other team members, and drove to Indiana for a weekend of meetings. My car was rear-ended in Indianapolis and we were unable to open the trunk to access our clothes for the program at a church that evening. Our quartet performed in our grungy clothes and I don't think Bob Stacy was thrilled with our appearance.

I really appreciated my classes under Brother Stacy and the experience I gained working with him and his High School Assembly Team. That experience proved very helpful when I began conducting high school assemblies on my own during the years I traveled with Operation Evangelize Ministries.

Jenny Sue is Summoned Home

Shortly after the beginning of the second semester of our freshman year, Jenny Sue's father was involved in an automobile accident. One very cold night, he ran off US 31 in Franklin and his car crashed into other cars at a used car lot. The crash left her father unconscious, hanging out of the driver's side door of his car. Since his car was not visible from the highway, her father was not discovered until the next day. Jenny Sue was summoned home to help with her father's recovery. I definitely missed Jenny Sue that semester. About the same time, I moved into an apartment house with some of my buddies from college. The house was midway between the college and my job. Since I did not have a car, this arrangement saved me a lot of walking. I made memories to last a lifetime living with my buddies in that apartment house.

Jenny Sue came to visit during the second semester of my freshman year and we became engaged. I asked her to marry me sitting in the swing on the front porch of the apartment house where I lived with my buddies. We picked out rings at Zale's Jewelry in Joplin and put them in lay-away. My mother, who was working at the G.C. Murphy Department Store in Franklin, Indiana, sent a little money each month to help me pay for them. I still wear my original wedding band, but fifty-nine years of wear has worn the decorative finish to a smooth finish and I had to have the ring cut off and enlarged several years ago. Jenny Sue had the original diamonds from her engagement and wedding rings set in a new band a few years back, so our wedding bands or portions thereof, have lasted fifty-nine years. Much like our marriage, they are worn, repaired, but intact.

Back Home Again in Indiana

At the close of my first year at OBC, I said goodbye to my college friends and the people at Smith's Paint Store and returned home to Indiana for the summer. It was good to be home with my family and Jenny Sue. It was also a learning experience, because I was asked to serve as Youth Minister at Franklin Memorial Church, even though I knew very little about youth ministry. One of the highlights of that summer was ministering with a Mexican student from a Bible College in Texas. His name was Juvanal and he had been hired by a group of area churches to minister to people who lived in migrant camps and worked in area canning factories. I received a crash course in Spanish, a greater understanding of Mexican culture, and a lot of valuable cross-cultural ministry experience.

About six months before the summer break from college, I was asked to preach at Franklin Memorial when I returned home. This would be my first sermon and, fortunately, I had six months to pre-pare. My first sermon was very stressful. Public speaking had never been one of my strong points. When required to make a speech in high school, I usually locked-up with stage fright. The week before I preached at Franklin Memorial, I developed diarrhea and nausea. I remember standing at the front door of the church, welcoming people to the service, feeling as if I were going to throw up or soil my pants. Sweat was running down my back and my face. I gave it my best shot and preached just about everything I knew in twenty minutes. People congratulated me at the close of the service, but I was not sure I was going to make it in the ministry. One lady, who had lived near me when I was a kid, exclaimed loudly, "Oh, Donnie Whetstine, I still remember when you killed my chicken"! This lady once had a fat old hen that ran loose in the neighborhood and I climbed to the top of our shed and tossed it off to see if it could fly. It died shortly thereafter. I was pretty humiliated that she reminded me of that incident right after I preached my first sermon. I preached at Franklin Memorial a couple more times that summer and grew more confident each time. I also began to depend more on the anointing of the Holy Spirit and less on me.

As payment for serving as Youth Minister, the minister of Franklin Memorial had promised me a hefty offering at the close of the summer, but the minister was fired and that hefty offering did not materialize. This meant that I would return to OBC broke and have to find a job before enrolling. Franklin Memorial did fulfill their promise to pay for my tuition and books, which was a huge blessing.

HOMELESS IN JOPLIN MISSOURI

Like the previous year, I arrived in Joplin a week before school started to hunt for a job. I had saved some money that I used for food, but I did not have enough money to rent a place to live. I found a job sacking groceries at a Safeway Supermarket, but was basically homeless. Another student returned under similar circumstances and, luckily, we had brought our sleeping bags and we were resourceful. There was a large awning that hung over the steps of the OBC Administration Building, which was still in use as the college was in the process of moving to its new campus. A steel ladder attached to the awning, served as a fire escape when the women's dorm was located on the second floor of the building. My friend and I climbed up the ladder and stashed our sleeping bags and other belongings on the awning. That is where we slept for several nights. Fortunately, there was a two foot knee wall around the edge of the awning, which provided some privacy and it didn't rain. My outdoorsman spirit was quite content with our housing arrangement. My friend and I were kindred spirits, for he had also grown up poor and was a man of the outdoors. Today, I look back on my homeless experience in Joplin and smile. Recently, I asked my friend if he remembered that experience. He said no, but I do and it is a good memory.

Jenny Sue arrived in Joplin and we enrolled in college. I had found a place to stay and Jenny Sue moved into the women's dorm on the new campus. As students returned to college, we found ourselves surrounded by good friends from our freshman year. All was well!

Desiring to Preach

Working at Safeway Supermarket was a God-send, but I really wanted to preach. There were numerous churches in the Joplin area that hired students from the college as part time ministers. Those churches were referred to as "preaching points". I needed a car to get to a preaching point and Jenny Sue and I began to pray about that. A good friend was hired at a church in Kansas, but was able to continue his education at OBC, traveling to Kansas on weekends to serve his church. He was paid well enough to buy a new car and, knowing I needed a car, he sold his 1955 Chrysler New Yorker to me for ONE dollar. Now, I was able to search for a preaching point. I actually found two preaching points and became the Minister of Prairie View Christian Church and Abo Christian Church, both located near Lebanon, Missouri, about a two hour drive from Joplin. We used to joke that an OBC student preacher's spirituality was gauged by how far he drove on the weekend to preach. My four hour round trip ranked me near the top.

I preached at Prairie View Sunday morning and evening and at Abo every other Sunday afternoon. Families from Prairie View took us into their homes and fed us quite well. Prairie View was, as the name implied, situated on the prairie near Lebanon. Jenny Sue received permission to travel to those ministries with me and get back after dorm hours. She sometimes led singing at Prairie View and Abo.

Mr. Vanhooser was an unforgettable member of the Prairie View church. He was nearly deaf and seldom looked up as he thundered out the hymns with his deep bass voice. We soon learned that it was useless to tell the congregation which verse of a hymn we would sing next. We just waited to see which verse Mr. Vanhooser chose and joined him.

One of the members of Prairie View lived directly across a field from the church building. On nice days, he rode a horse to church and tied it to a fence post next to the building. That horse could evidently tell time, because when it was time for me to conclude my sermon, it would begin banging its head against a feed sign that hung on the fence. I didn't need a wrist watch to know it was time to conclude my sermon. I just listened for the horse to bang the feed sign.

Abo was a little further East of Lebanon, located in the foothills of the Ozark Mountains. The drive to the church was beautiful. We crossed the Gasconade River and, in that day, the Gasconade was one of the best smallmouth bass streams in the country. We also saw huge flocks of turkeys on our drive to the church. A bird had flown into a window of the church building and broken a pane, where wasps entered and built nests on the ceiling. A woodstove was used to heat the building and when the room heated, the wasps came out and began to fly around. Some of church members were quite adept at slamming a song book shut on the wasps and I ducked the wasps as I preached. I have very good memories of the year we spent ministering at Prairie View and Abo. Several years ago, I trailered my Harley to Bennett Springs State Park near Lebanon to camp and search for those churches. I was sad to find that neither of those churches still exists, but the memories do.

Saying I Do

During Christmas break of our second year of college, Jenny Sue and I traveled home to Indiana to get married at Franklin Memorial Church. Since I was not yet twenty-one, I was required to have my parents sign for me to be married. As the law was written, Jenny Sue did not need her parents to sign. We also had to go before a judge to get the three day waiting period waived, so that we could get married while we were home for Christmas break. It all worked out and we were married on Christmas Eve in 1963. The minister of Franklin Memorial did the ceremony and Don Knoy, the minister who had baptized me, sang. I don't remember many details about the ceremony, but I do remember Don Knoy singing "Whither Thou Goest I will Go" and I remember Jenny Sue looking radiant in the wedding dress she fashioned herself. We got married in a blizzard and no one braved the elements to decorate our car. At the conclusion of the ceremony, Jenny Sue and I were exhausted and hungry. Since it was Christmas Eve and we were experiencing a blizzard, most of the restaurants were closed. We finally found a drive-in restaurant open, where we ate greasy burgers and fries. We slowly drove five miles through the blizzard to spend our wedding night in the bridal sweet of the Wishing Well Motel in Whiteland, Indiana. That motel still exists and looks just about as cheesy as it did back then.

Before we traveled to Indiana to be married, we rented a furnished apartment on North Joplin Street. It was an upstairs apartment with a combined living room and kitchenette, a bedroom, and a bath. What more do newlyweds need? We paid forty dollars a month for the apartment. Some of my buddies were envious that we were married and had a place of our own. It was pretty special!

At the close of our second year at OBC, we had to leave Prairie View and Abo because Prairie View was short on funds and could no longer pay a preacher. We couldn't afford to travel four hours round trip without compensation. OBC received regular requests for preachers to fill-in at area churches. The college called it "supply preaching". I began supply preaching on Sundays, while searching for another part time ministry. Don Earl Boatman, the president of OBC, was very helpful in linking student preachers with potential churches for part time ministries. His help was greatly appreciated.

A New Ministry

During the time I was searching for a part time ministry, the Schell City Christian Church asked me to come for an interview and preach a trial sermon. I was hired! Schell City was located eighty miles northeast of Joplin and a hundred miles southeast of Kansas City. The first time we drove into Schell City, Jenny Sue and I began humming the theme song to the Twilight Zone. It was like stepping back in time. The business district in this old Missouri farming town had high sidewalks with the remains of hitching posts, where people had once tied their horses. Except for the main highway that ran through town, the streets of the town were gravel, which turned to mud when it rained. The church people were very friendly and we began making lasting friendships. The church ran about a hundred in attendance on Sunday mornings and they were able to pay me well enough that I no longer needed to work at the supermarket. The ministry at Schell City was as close to a fulltime ministry as I could have had as a Bible College student and I gained valuable experience that served me well in later ministries.

The church rented a house in town that served as the parsonage for the Minister. It was an old two story house, with no running water. There was a hand pump on the kitchen sink that pumped water from a well under the house and a gas stove for cooking. The parsonage came complete with a two-hole outhouse that had carpet and wallpaper.

The main source of heat was a woodstove, but the old house was so drafty that it was very hard to keep warm. During the summer months, the old house was a delight. There was a fenced garden area where we raised vegetables and the trees and shrubbery around the house attracted many song birds. Jenny Sue and I spent Friday night thru Sunday in the parsonage and returned to Joplin on Monday morning. OBC did not have classes on Monday to allow preachers to travel to and from their weekend ministries. I was very thankful for that.

After my first year at Schell City, the church bought a Spartan Trailer to serve as a parsonage and parked it next to the church. At last Jenny Sue and I had running water and a flushing toilet. We felt like we were truly living the dream! After we had served a year in Schell City, we were unable to pay both the utilities for the trailer and the rent for our apartment in Joplin, so we agreed that Jenny Sue would live fulltime in Schell City and I would commute to Joplin to finish college. Jenny Sue got a job at a shirt factory in Eldorado Springs and rode to work with a couple of women in the church, who also worked at the shirt factory. She tells that me it was a hard place to work, because some of the women who worked in the factory were mean. I drove to Joplin on Tuesday morning for classes and returned on Friday evening. When I got home on Friday evening, we ate home-made tacos and listened to Tijuana Brass music. It was our special tradition.

AUNT EM AND MRS STEPHENSON

Soon after I began ministering in Schell City, I was told that the previous minister visited a homebound church member each Sunday afternoon, to share his Sunday morning message with her. Jenny Sue and I gladly agreed to do the same and began visiting her each Sunday afternoon. Known to everyone as Aunt Em, she had been bedfast for several years, after having a leg amputated. She lived with her adult son, who assisted her. Aunt Em was a delight and Jenny Sue and I gained as much from our visits as she did from us. Aunt Em was 97 years old and had come west to Missouri in a covered wagon as a child. I never grew tired of hearing her fascinating stories.

Aunt Em's elderly sister, Mrs. Stephenson, lived a few blocks away, but the sisters never visited, because Mrs. Stephenson was also bedfast. Like Aunt Em, Mrs. Stephenson was a delight. I visited her weekly and prayed with her. Mrs. Stephenson moved from talking to me and talking to Jesus so easily that I felt like Jesus was present in the room —I think He was.

One warm afternoon, another lady in the church and I lifted Aunt Em into her wheelchair and took her to see her sister. I cannot adequately put into words what happened when these two sisters met. They laughed and wept as they hugged and kissed each other profusely. I still remember one of the sisters saying, "I didn't think I would see you again until we got to heaven". That was one of the best things I ever did in my entire ministry! Both of the sisters passed away while I ministered in Schell City and I preached their funerals. I can only imagine the greeting they had in Heaven.

HIGH SCHOOL BASEBALL AND THE SOFTBALL LEAGUE

I connected easily with the teens in the church and in the community, because I wasn't much older. I became good friends with the man who coached baseball and basketball at the high school, who was also the minister of the Methodist Church in town. Occasionally, when the coach was short a player for the high school baseball team, he would call on me. I still remember playing second base and Jenny Sue keeping score at a game in a nearby town. No one ever questioned my age. The coach and I started a softball league in Schell City that was a huge success. Churches, businesses, and service clubs started teams to play in the league. We raised money to buy lights for the baseball field at the high school where we played our games. The Christian Church had a team in the league and I was the pitcher. We had some great times playing in the softball league during the summers. The townspeople sat in the grandstands or parked their cars along the street next to the softball field. The people in their cars would honk their horns when a run scored, or when they liked a play. The games were played late into the night. I remember going home one night after our team had played and hearing car horns until midnight. Yep, the Schell City softball league was a huge success!

SUCCESSFUL MINISTRY

We saw many people come to Christ in those years at Schell City. VBS was always a big success, as well as our youth groups and Sunday morning services. We had several successful revival meetings while we were there. A meeting with John Lytle preaching was very memorable. For some reason John declined to stay the week with us in the old parsonage with the outhouse. He decided instead to drive to and from his home in Diamond, Missouri each day. Good call John! I also worked with John in camp at Cyokamo Christian Camp, where the youth from Schell City attended summer camp. Years later, John preached a couple of revival meetings at the Nashville Christian Church, while I was the minister. John was at that time ministering in Sullivan, Indiana. The people in Nashville loved John as much as the people in Schell City. I did too. He was a good brother, a good friend.

I asked Joe Garman and a team of singers from OBC to come to Schell City to conduct a youth revival one spring. It turned out to be one of the most successful revivals we had. The building was packed each night and several teens accepted Christ and were baptized.

Schell City was a sportsman's paradise for people who loved to hunt and fish. I hunted ducks, rabbits, squirrels, deer, and quail. I also caught fish and picked blackberries and mushrooms. We ate a lot of wild stuff while we lived in Schell City.

I drove through Schell City a few years ago on my return home from a camping trip out west. It was sad to see how run-down the town had become. The high school was boarded-up, the softball field was gone, and the buildings of the business district were deserted and falling down. The Schell City Christian Church was still there and had actually built an addition onto the building. All that is left of Schell City, as we knew it back in the late 60's, is the memories. They are good and I plan to keep them!

A LIFE-CHANGING EXPERIENCE

I had a life-changing experience that could have been a life-ending experience the last year I ministered in Schell City. During my final year at OBC, I had to arise at 0-dark-thirty on Tuesday morning to make the hour and a half drive to Joplin for a 7 AM class. One cold winter morning, I went to sleep at the wheel, just before I crossed the Spring River. I awoke just in time to avoid plunging over the ravine into the Spring River and certain death. I yanked the car back on the road and slid halfway through the Spring River Bridge. I was so shaken that I pulled my car to the side of the road to regain my composure. It was then I recalled being awakened by someone loudly shouting my name, but I was alone in the car. At that point in my life, my theology said that God no longer spoke to people, but only speaks through the Bible. Nonetheless, I was totally aware that God had just messed with my theology big time, by speaking to me! I can't say for certain that it was an audible voice, since I was asleep. I can't be certain that it was God or an Angel, since I was asleep. But, of one thing I am certain, God spoke to me and I am happy that He did!

That experience birthed a lifelong quest to discover how God speaks to me. Jesus did say that His sheep hear his voice. After fifty years of learning to discern God's voice in my spirit, I am absolutely convinced that God still speaks to his followers. But, lest I violate a promise that I made in the introduction of this book to not "grind any theological axes", I will move on. However, there are several stories in this book that reveal how God has spoken to me very dramatically through the years.

Graduation and
Departing Missouri

In the spring of 1967, I graduated from Ozark Bible College (today called Ozark Christian College) with a Bachelor of Sacred Literature degree. I am very thankful for the education that I received at OBC, the professors who inspired and befriended me, and the many students who became lifelong friends. It was a great experience! I was sad to say good bye to my friends at OBC and at Schell City, but I had graduated and it was time to move on. My mom and dad came to Missouri to help us pack and move out of our cute little Spartan Trailer to head to Indiana.

Shortly before I graduated, I was contacted by an Indianapolis church and asked to become their minister. So, I left the ministry at the Schell City Christian Church to become the Minister of the Mars View Christian Church on the southwest side of Indianapolis. Two of my buddies from OBC were hired at churches nearby, which was a blessing.

MY FIRST FULLTIME MINISTRY

This was my first fulltime ministry and I pursued it passionately. Soon after I began, I drove to a place that overlooked the area and prayed that God would allow me to see a harvest of souls there. And, I did what I knew to do, I started preaching about Jesus and knocking on doors. I still remember Seth Wilson exhorting young preachers, "Young men, preach Jesus"! That's what I did! Mars View had recently purchased a ranch style home in a nearby subdivision to serve as a parsonage. Jenny Sue and I moved in and began making friends in the neighborhood.

Shortly after I began preaching at Mars View, I concluded my sermon with an illustration about John Dillinger that left the congregation deathly quiet. As I walked to the back of the sanctuary to speak to people as they left, the elders were waiting and ushered me into the church office. They told me I needed to know that John Dillinger's sister was a member of the church. Wow, I had never been more blown-away! Luckily, John's sister, a very sweet lady, was not there that Sunday. Through the years, she and I had several interesting conversations about her notorious brother.

LIFE IN THE SUBDIVISION

Jenny Sue and I befriended a couple who lived across the street from the parsonage with their three young children. Eddie and Doris did not attend church and never came to ours, but they were our friends. We loved them and spent time with them. Eddie and I had similar interests. We bought mini bikes and rode them all over the fields behind the parsonage. I prayed for Eddie a lot, but he did not express interest in being a Christian. After we left Indianapolis, I lost contact with Eddie and Doris, but reconnected with Eddie almost fifty years later via Face Book. He shared that he and Doris divorced and she passed away. That was sad. A couple of years into our FB friendship, Eddie told me he was dying of COPD and asked me to preach his funeral. I went to visit Eddie and his new wife and shared the Gospel with him. Eddie's wife and I urged Eddie to trust Christ as his Savior and, fifty years after I first met Eddie, I prayed with him to receive Christ as his Savior. I remain friends with two of Eddie's children via Face Book.

We loved the little ranch style house on Murray Avenue in the Maywood Manor subdivision. Behind our house were farm fields, woodlands, and abandoned gravel pits, all the way back to the White River. Even though I lived in the city, I had quick access to the country. I hunted rabbits with my Beagle Hound, fished, and explored. It was the perfect situation for a city preacher, who was an outdoorsman. We raised a vegetable garden and had a nice little patio in our back yard. Life was good!

GROWING IN SPITE OF OBSTACLES

Mars View was a church of about a hundred people, most of whom were really sweet people, but there was a group of disagreeable people in the church who made my ministry difficult. I organized a calling program and, as we canvassed the neighborhood, new people came to our services almost every Sunday. However, the disagreeable people ran some of them off. That was frustrating. An argument erupted at almost every church board meeting. In spite of this, the church grew and people were accepting Christ and being baptized regularly.

A Divine Appointment at the Wrong Address

One night as I was sending out the calling teams, I gave an address to a couple of men and asked them to call on a family who had shown interest in our church. They went to the wrong address, but returned to say that the family they accidently visited, was interested in attending our church. I followed-up and shared the Gospel with the family, eventually baptizing the whole family. Bill, the father, and I became instant friends. We regularly hunted, fished and played golf together. Bill was an electrician and worked with high voltage electricity at a local factory. He always said that he would only make one mistake. Several years after I left Mars View, he made that one mistake and died by electrocution. I was very sad when I heard about Bill's death. Fifty years later, I remain friends with Bill's son, Bill Jr.

We had a wonderful group of young couples in the church and we met together for fellowship and Bible study. We saw a lot of spiritual growth in those couples. Our youth groups also grew, especially the teenage group. Our youth attended camp at Allendale Christian Assembly, so I usually accompanied them to camp and served in different capacities. I had some great experiences at Allendale.

OUR FIRSTBORN

Our son Brent was born while we ministered at Mars View. Jenny Sue gave birth to Brent at the old Saint Vincent Hospital in Indianapolis. Brent was a happy baby. From the time we brought him home from the hospital, he slept eight hours a night and awoke cooing and playing with the mobile that hung over his crib. Jenny Sue and I loved to camp and we began taking Brent on overnight camping trips when he was six weeks old. When Brent was six months old, we took him on a week-long camping trip to the Smoky Mountains. One day, Jenny Sue walked up the trail from our campsite to fetch water and left Brent and I napping in the tent. I awoke to find a Black Bear standing in the tent looking at me. I sat up quickly and yelled at the bear, which ran up the trail as Jenny Sue was returning with water. She thought the bear was attacking her and really freaked-out. I am very happy that the bear didn't attack Jenny Sue or eat Brent. I think they are happy about that too.

THOSE WHO KNOW, SAY RENAULT

While I was ministering in Indy, I bought a used Renault, which was France's answer to Germany's Volkswagen Beetle. The Renault seated four people and had a rear-mounted engine. It got great gas mileage and, in 1967, I could fill the tank for two dollars and fifty cents—yes, you read that correctly! Looking back, I think it was a piece of junk, but it was a cute little piece of junk. I repaired the body and repainted it, so it looked pretty nice. One day when I was making calls, I blew a head gasket and barely made it home. It was winter, we didn't have a garage, and it was too cold to overhaul the engine in my driveway, so I did the work in the kitchen of the parsonage. I have always been a DIY guy. Parts were back ordered, so the engine sat in the kitchen for a couple of months. I was probably the only minister in Indy who had a Renault engine sitting in their kitchen. I eventually got the car back together and continued to use it to make ministerial calls. In the morning, I never knew where I would find that car, because it was so light that the neighborhood kids picked it up and carried it to different locations.

Officer Ray

One of the members of Mars View was an Indianapolis Police Officer named was Ray. After a messy divorce, Ray dropped out of church and drifted from God. He came back to the Lord and the church, about the time Jenny Sue and I arrived. Ray was great guy, very friendly, always joking, and fun to be around. He also had a good voice and sang in the choir. One evening, Ray ran off the Interstate, rolled his Pontiac Convertible, and was killed. That was a very sad time for our church and Ray's family. Ray's viewing was held at a local funeral home. Before the huge crowd of mourners arrived, I accompanied Ray's parents to the funeral home to view their son's body and grieve with them. Ray's parents grieved very hard! I tried my best to comfort them, but it was an impossible task. Ray's funeral was held the following day at Mars View Christian Church. The building was small and was packed to overflowing. In fact, I think there were as many people on the lawn as there were in the building. There was a huge police presence at the funeral. I spoke at Ray's funeral and then rode in the hearse to the cemetery, where Ray was buried. The funeral procession passed the City County Building in downtown Indianapolis, which was the headquarters of the Indianapolis Police Department. Hundreds of Police Officers lined both sides of the street in front of the City County Building. They stood in dress uniforms, saluting as the hearse passed. I choked-up as we passed them.

It was an unforgettable sight. I flashed back to that event a few years ago, as I stood in my Brown County Sheriff's Department uniform to salute an officer from our department, who had passed. No one honors their dead better than Law Enforcement and Military!

BROTHER BY A DIFFERENT MOTHER

A young man named Ron took special interest in my ministry, so I began to include him in my visitations. We also fished, hunted, and played golf together. Ron became as close to me as my own brother and he and his wife spent a lot of time at our house. Ron's brother came home from Vietnam suffering from PTSD. He, like many other Veterans, self-medicated with alcohol. Sometimes Ron's brother would disappear for days and he would ask me to help find him. This usually meant combing the bars on the east side of Indy. Once we found Ron's brother passed-out drunk on a pool table in a bar on east Washington Street, with a snow tire on each arm. The bartender said that he came in with the snow tires. When he sobered-up, we asked him where he got the snow tires and he didn't have a clue.

Ron and I hunted deer on a farm in Brown County that belonged to good friends of my family. The wife had helped deliver me. Ron worked at a grain co-op in Beech Grove and, after Ron got off work on Friday evening, we would drive to Brown County to camp and hunt deer. Those are good memories. After I left Indy to minister at the Nashville Christian Church, Ron went through a divorce and I lost contact with him. Later, I attempted to reconnect with Ron online and found his obituary. That was a sad day.

I have a lot of good memories of our ministry at Mars View and life in the subdivision. I also have some not so good memories caused by the disagreeable folk in the church.

THIS IS NOT BEA FERRELL'S YEAST ROLES!

I had some preconceived ideas about ministry that were formed at Franklin Memorial Church when I was young. My early years of ministry began to challenge those ideas. I remember the great fellowship, the encouragement I received, and the outstanding pitch-in dinners at Franklin Memorial. Bea Ferrell usually brought homemade yeast rolls that were to die for. Unconsciously, I think I believed that ministry would be like a long extended pitch-in dinner featuring Bea Ferrell's yeast rolls. Though ministry was at times very pleasant and included some great fellowship, other times were unpleasant. I was not prepared for that. I am sure that Franklin Memorial had underlying problems when I was young, but since I was not in leadership, I was sheltered from them. As a Minister, I became very aware of the common conflicts in churches.

All churches have problems, even churches in the New Testament. Many of the Epistles in the New Testament were written partly to correct problems in the churches. I soon found that when problems arose in the church, the buck stopped at the preacher's desk, my desk! I was often saddled with the responsibility of correcting problems in the church, the nature of which ranged from simple to ridiculous. I learned one valuable lesson in those years. You don't have to fight every fire that ignites in the church. Some fires will burn-out on their own and it's best to just pray and let them burn-out. If you decide that a fire is worth fighting, expect to get burned a little in the process.

I also learned about "they". I was often unable to identify who "they" were, but "they" were unhappy and "they" expected me to address the problem. I would like to have a dollar for every time a church leader informed me that "they" were unhappy about something. My standard response was to ask who "they" were and the standard answer was, "Well, I can't say, but "they" are unhappy". Geesh, this was not Bea Ferrell's yeast rolls! Ministry was a bit harder than I imagined.

Moving On

After three years at Mars View, I was ready to minister somewhere else. During that period of disillusionment, I preached a revival at a church in Kentucky. My friend Dave Woods, minister of the church, grew up in Brown County. I met Dave at Allendale Christian Assembly when I was a freshman in college and he was in high school. Dave told me that his home church, the Nashville Christian Church, was looking for a minister. He said that he would recommend me, if I was interested. I had always dreamed of living in Brown County where both my parents were born. Yes, I was interested in talking with the leaders of the Nashville church! After interviewing with the leaders of the church, they came to Mars View to hear me preach. The leaders at Mars View suspected that this group of men was a pulpit committee and took me aside to ask if I was planning to leave and I told them that I was. Shortly after, I preached a trial sermon at the Nashville Christian Church and was hired. One lady did not vote for me and told me that she preferred an older man. I was twenty-six years old.

Coming Home to a Place I had Never Lived Before

Some of my earliest memories involve Brown County. I remember traveling with my family to Oscar and Ellie Smith's primitive farm on Beck's Grove Road every summer to celebrate their birthdays. Oscar was my mother's brother. Ellie was mute, but communicated with gestures and sounds that you soon began to recognize. She was a sweet, affectionate lady. They had a very small house with no running water, so tables and chairs were set-up in the yard for eating pitch-in style. After eating, my Uncle Jim usually started a Euchre game, the ladies sat and talked, and the kids explored the farm. Oscar farmed with mules and also had chickens, goats, cows, and a horde of primitive farming equipment. Oscar's farm was a magical place that I never grew tired of exploring.

My Uncle Will and Aunt Story had a farm on Upper Salt Creek. In those days, there were few bridges over the creeks on the back roads of Brown County, so we drove through the creeks. Uncle Will and Aunt Story's drive went through the creek, which I found fascinating. They also had a footbridge suspended on cables, which was used when the water was high. When our family visited Uncle Will and Aunt Story, my brother and I roamed the woods, played in the creek, and had grand adventures. The first time I saw a Timber Rattler was at

Uncle Will's farm. I was wading in the creek and looked up to see a huge Timber Rattler coiled on the bank at eye level. I nearly splashed all the water out of the creek running away.

When I was young, Memorial Day was called Decoration Day. On Decoration Day, the extended family traveled to the Gnawbone Cemetery to clean and decorate the graves of my mother's relatives. The men brought saw horses and boards to make tables for eating and tools for cleaning the cemetery. The ladies brought food for meals and flowers to decorate graves. That's where we young people learned the history of our Brown County ancestors. The adults led us through the cemetery, pointing to graves and telling stories about our relatives. My older sister says that I once wandered away on Decoration Day and it was quite a while before I was found. I was so young that I have no memory of the event. I will blame my big sister for being lost, since she was supposed to be watching me. Lol! I have mentioned elsewhere in this book about fishing and hunting trips to Brown County with my dad and other relatives. Brown County was a sacred place to me.

Just after Christmas in 1969, Jenny Sue, six month old Brent, and I moved into the parsonage next to Nashville Christian Church. It was a cold day with almost a foot of snow on the ground, but that did not dampen our enthusiasm. I felt like I had come home to a place where I had never lived before, the place of my ancestors, the place I had always dreamed of living.

Brown County Ministry

I have many good memories of my five years of ministry in Nashville, but I will attempt to practice brevity. At the beginning of my ministry at the church, attendance averaged one hundred eighty-five people per Sunday. After five years, attendance grew to two hundred thirty-five. All ages were represented in the congregation, from the elderly to infants in the nursery.

One of the infants in the nursery was our daughter Sharianne, born while we ministered in Nashville. I was told that Jenny Sue had begun labor, while I was playing softball with our church team. I hurried home to drive Jenny Sue to the hospital in Franklin to deliver Sharianne by C-section. In those days, husbands were not allowed in the surgery room, so I sat nervously in the waiting room. After a short forty-five minute wait, a nurse came out to tell me that we had a baby girl. Since ultrasounds were not available in those days, we did not know the sex of the baby and were convinced that we would have another boy. I built Brent's bed, which I planned to turn into a trundle bed to sleep two boys.

When I learned that we had a girl, my first words were, "Well, I guess it won't be a trundle bed"!

While in Nashville, I worked with several part time youth ministers, Bible college students from Cincinnati, who served our church on weekends. Dale was one of my favorites. A friendly Kentucky boy, he always wore a big grin and greeted you with, "Howdy"! Dale oversaw our children's church and youth groups and often accompanied me when I made calls. We became good friends and worked well together. Even though we had a youth minister, I spent a lot of time ministering to the teens in our church, who hung out at the parsonage. We played ping pong in the basement and, back in the day, I was pretty much unbeatable. I had many challengers!

I really enjoyed interacting with the leaders of the church, who often went calling with me. That was good time spent together in ministry. They were good men, sincere Christians, and I was blessed by time shared with them.

The elderly people in our church were a delight and I loved spending time with them. They were artists, authors, teachers, and people from many other professions, who had come to Brown County to retire. Famous artist Carey Cloud, was a member of our church. He gave our kids some of the original toys that he had developed for boxes of Cracker Jacks. He was a true gentleman and a delight to be around. The elderly members of our church had interesting stories to tell and I love stories!

Jenny Sue and I became good friends with many of the young couples in the church and started a small group with them. We met weekly in different couple's homes to study the Bible, pray, and fellowship. We also planned special outings and campouts. This was one of the most successful small groups I have ever been involved with and we saw a lot of spiritual growth in its members. We were more than just a small group, we became family. We remain friends with many of them almost fifty years later.

I cannot recount how many people I baptized, married, or buried during my five years at the Nashville Christian Church. I will be forever grateful that God led us to the ministry in Nashville and to the many people who were our friends and comrades. I was twenty-six years old when I began my ministry with the church and thirty-one when I left. Man, I was young!

MOVED BY THE JESUS MOVEMENT

O ne of the greatest influences upon my life was the Jesus
Movement, which broke out in the late 60s, just about the time
Jenny Sue and I began our ministry in Nashville. The Jesus Movement
began on the beaches of California and sent shock waves around the
world. Young people from across the nation began to come alive spiritually and the teens in our church did too. The teens chose to sit in the
front rows of the church, right in front of the pulpit. When I prayed
during the Sunday morning service, they dropped to their knees. It
was very touching and hard to ignore, since they were at the front of
the sanctuary.

There was a lot of fellowship and shared ministry between the
teens in the area churches in those days. A church in Columbus started
a meeting for teens called TNT—Thursday Night Thing. TNT was
a huge success, attracting a large group of teens from area churches. I
usually attended those meetings with our teens and I was inspired as
much as they were. The meetings included group singing, testimonies,
and encouragement from area ministers and youth workers. Some of
the testimonies were unforgettable.

The teens from our church were great witnesses for Christ at our
local high school. A disagreement once broke out in a class over the
teaching of evolution. The teacher suggested a debate, with a couple of
the teens of opposing viewpoints speaking on the subject. Then, the

class was to vote for the most credible view. One of the teens from our church was selected to present her views on creation and did a superb job. Another student presented his argument for evolution and the class voted almost unanimously that creation was the most credible view. The teacher was upset and invited a professor from Indiana University to come to the school and present a lecture on evolution to the whole student body. Some of the teens from our church, were stationed at the entrances to the gymnasium where the lecture was held, handing out a very interesting cartoon type tract on creation entitled, "Big Daddy". Guess what the students were doing while the University Professor was delivering his boring speech?

During those days, I began gathering a group of teens on Sunday afternoons to witness on the streets of Nashville. Nashville, a tourist town, was filled with people every weekend, including many teens. It was a perfect place to share Jesus! We held a prayer time in the front yard of the parsonage and then walked the streets of Nashville passing-out tracts and sharing Jesus with the tourists.

With all that Jesus fervor, weeks of Christian camp turned into youth revivals. To this day, when I walk across the campus of Hilltop Christian Camp in Brown County, I am filled with memories of life-changing encounters with young people. Stuff was happening and it was good! I began to encounter a shift in the direction of my ministry. The winds of change were blowing.

As I write this section of the book in February of 2023, there are indications that we may be on the threshold of another outpouring similar to the Jesus Movement. Oh, how my heart longs for that!

NEW DIRECTION

I invited Don Todd to the church to conduct a revival, where we saw many people come to Christ. Don also went to our local high school to hold an assembly for the young people. Don played a Martin 12-string guitar, which fascinated me. After that, I wanted to learn to play guitar, so I bought a cheap, very cheap, guitar from Sears, which included an instruction book and began to teach myself to play guitar. My early attempts to play guitar were almost as crude as my Sears guitar, but I soon replaced that piece of wood with a Greco 12-string guitar and my guitar playing actually began to sound like music. The more I played, the more requests I received to play at local churches and youth events. That 12-string guitar accompanied me to many weeks of camp, where playing around camp fires probably shortened its life considerably. In those days, people began to tell me I had missed my calling and should be working with young people. Hmmm!

Something else happened at that time which was a bit life-changing. I walked into a leather shop in Nashville, which was operated by my hippie friends Dave and Cliff. Though good friends, I never knew their last names, because hippies didn't use last names. Last names represented "The Man", or the establishment and hippies were anti-establishment. My friends were playing a Christian rock and roll album and I had never heard anything like it, so I asked, "Who is that"?! My friends answered, "Oh, that's Larry Norman, man"! It was one of Larry's first albums, entitled "Upon This Rock". I was hooked and I have remained a fan of Larry's music ever since. In the late 60s and early 70s, a new style of music was fueling the Jesus Movement and I liked it. I began learning to play and sing many of the songs that I heard from Christian Rock groups that were popping up everywhere.

SPEAKING OF HIPPIES

A local man, who had married into a lot of money, embraced the hippie lifestyle and bought several hundred acres of land in Brown County, where he developed a hippie commune near Needmore. During the May Day Demonstration in Washington, DC, he recruited a large group of hippies to come to Needmore. In the late 60s and early 70s, the local commune was frequented by some of the major leaders of the hippie/peace movement. If you were a hippie, Needmore was the place to be. Through the years, people often called me a hippie, probably because of my minimalist lifestyle and my long hair. I was fascinated with the hippies and began to befriend them. I have often said that I never met a hippie that I didn't like and the same is true for bikers. Many of the hippies were craftsman, who worked with wood, leather, and pottery. Dave and Cliff, my leather-working friends, said that you should not work to make money, but to be fulfilled. I liked that! In fact, I liked a lot of the philosophies embraced by the hippies.

A hippie preacher, who traveled the circuit of communes preaching about Jesus, came to Needmore in the early 70s. This long-haired, bearded, preacher was a solid Christian and an amazing preacher. He began holding meetings at the commune and lives were transformed. Hippies, who had attended the May Day Demonstration, were especially impacted by this man's preaching. Those folk believed that the May Day Demonstration was going to make a significant impact on the corrupt American system. Instead, they left the event feeling discouraged and disillusioned. Their hearts were fallow ground for the Gospel.

As a result of this man's preaching, a large group of hippies accepted Christ and wanted to be baptized. A couple of my friends, who were helping minister at the commune, asked if they could use the baptistry at the Christian Church. I asked the Elders of the church, who reluctantly gave permission, with one stipulation. I had to clean and refill the baptistry each time we baptized hippies. So, I got to take part in some of the most incredible baptisms that I have ever experienced, which was repeated several times in the coming months. Because of my acceptance of the hippies, they decided to worship with our church. They also decided that they should dress to reflect the fact that they had been born-again. The men buzzed-off their hair and wore suits to worship. The ladies wore nice dresses. There were no bandanas, beads, or tie dye. The hippies were some of the best dressed people in our worship service. Some of the people in our congregation were upset with me for ministering to hippies and baptizing them in our baptistry. Ironically, those disgruntled folks sat with the hippies in worship and didn't have a clue. Although, when the hippies raised their fist and shouted "right on" during my sermon, it was obvious that they were not part of the usual crowd of worshippers.

It became apparent that the hippies would be better served by a church at the commune. A group of us, who had been ministering to the hippies, met with the couple who led the commune to discuss starting a church. The couple was very interested, because they had recently given their lives to Christ. The night they were baptized, they burned all their illegal drugs in their fireplace. Anyone downwind probably got a contact buzz from the smoke.

So a church was birthed at the hippie commune in Needmore. It was not a traditional church by any means. It was loud, rowdy, and totally unpredictable, but always exciting. It brought together people who had been schooled by the communists to overthrow the government, Peaceniks, SDS members, people who were involved in witchcraft, and drug users of every variety. Jesus shined! Lives were transformed! People were delivered from witchcraft and addiction!

I became good friends with a hippie named Bruce. When I first met him, he was a speed freak. His hair was falling out and his skin looked like that of a corpse. When he undressed to be baptized, I could hardly stand the stench. Six months later, Bruce looked like a totally different person. He was clean, sober, healthy, and a powerful witness for Christ at the commune. Bruce was a gifted magician. He left the commune to pursue a career in magic as a means of sharing Christ.

I also remember Greg, who enthusiastically received Christ and was baptized. I wanted to give him a Bible, but I had given away almost every Bible that I owned. I did have a large ornate family Bible that sat on our coffee table. One of those Bibles that look nice, but you never actually read. I apologetically offered it to Greg and he said, "Far Out"! I smiled when I saw him proudly carrying that huge Bible on the streets of Nashville. Greg had dropped a lot of acid (LSD) and it had taken a toll on him. He struggled with flashbacks and mental lapses. Occasionally he would go blank, almost like he had fallen asleep with his eyes open. We would shake him and call his name and he would slowly respond. I had heard that memorizing Scripture was helpful in restoring the minds of former drug addicts. I suggested this to Greg and he began to memorize Scripture with a passion. Gradually, the memory lapses and flashbacks disappeared.

SEEKING A NEW WINESKIN

Jesus said that new wine will burst old wineskins, so it must be put in new wineskins. The new wine being produced by the Jesus Movement was stretching mainline churches to the bursting point. Many churches resisted it altogether, so a lot of evangelism during the Jesus Movement was taking place outside conventional churches. Churches that embraced the Jesus Movement grew dramatically as they accommodated this new wave of non-traditional Christians. Para Church Organizations were formed to work alongside churches to reach this new generation of believers. Also, many independent ministries sprang-up on college and high school campuses. Coffee houses, Christian festivals, and a new style of non-conventional church became part of the new wineskin to receive what was being produced by the Spirit. This exciting time in the history of American Christianity left an indelible mark on the American church. And, on me!

I felt God leading me to become part of this move of His Spirit and felt that He had been preparing me for this very thing through shifts that were occurring in my ministry. I began to pray for God to open a door to be involved. That's the way I have always sought God's direction; I pray and wait for Him to move.

A lady named Agnes and her husband Don lived near the commune and helped with the ministry. Agnes, a fearless servant of God, was rattled by nothing. She called one morning to tell me about a dream. In her dream she saw the vision of Ezekiel, recorded in Ezekiel chapter forty-seven, where a river flowed from the Temple of God through the Eastern Gate into the Arabah. The Scripture says the river grew deeper and wider as it flowed down to the Dead Sea, where the acrid water became fresh and teemed with fish. Agnes said she saw me in the dream, standing knee deep in the river. She concluded by saying that she didn't know what the dream meant, but thought I should pray about it. I thanked her for calling me and went straight to my knees. I knew exactly what Agnes' dream meant—I had been only wading in the flow of God's Spirit and He was calling me deeper.

As I was praying and waiting, our youth leaders urged me to invite Dave Lucas and the Watchmen Quartet to do a weekend of meetings at our church. Students at a Christian college in Kentucky, they were well known in area churches. I knew them from working with them at Hilltop Camp. I contacted Dave and the Watchmen and asked them to come to our church. It was very successful meeting and the building was packed for every service. Many decisions were made to follow Christ.

At the close of the weekend, Dave and one of the members of the Watchmen came to my house to share their plan to start a ministry called Operation Evangelize Youth Mission Incorporated. They excitedly shared their vision of evangelistic teams traveling across the country, working alongside churches to reach young people. Then, they asked if I would like to be part of this mission. I had been praying for God to open a door to do exactly that, so their offer looked like a door big enough to drive a Mack Truck through. I said yes!

New Beginning in a New Ministry

A generous member of a church in Chesapeake, Ohio sold Operation Evangelize (O.E.) two lots of property at a very reasonable price, which included two two-story houses and two one-story houses. The two-story houses were remodeled to become living quarters for team members. The two one-story houses became office space, a print shop, and some additional living space. Our ministry had a great partnership with the church, located next door to the property.

I wanted to buy a new van for my traveling ministry and friends of O.E., who owned a Dodge dealership, offered to sell one at cost. Jenny Sue and I began to pray for God to supply the funds. While we were praying, some close friends from the Nashville Christian Church asked to meet with us. They told us that God had moved them to provide the funds to buy our van. Whoohoo! What a blessing!

I busied myself converting the van into a camper, with space to store my musical equipment. We were also busy closing our ministry with the church in Nashville and making preparations to move to Ohio to live on the O.E. compound. It was exciting to be part of developing this brand new youth ministry and begin a new adventure in traveling ministry. Just before we moved, I traveled to Flora, Illinois to record my first music album entitled "Love One Another". The title song was written by my friend, June. June often stayed with Jenny Sue and I on weekends during her last couple of years of high school and we played guitar together a lot. In those days, we often had someone camping in the basement of the parsonage in Nashville. The album, a fun project, incorporated some of my musician friends, an excellent studio musician, and a few of the O.E. team members. We spent thirteen hours straight in the recording studio and returned to Indiana absolutely whipped. We couldn't rest for long, because the next day some of the O.E. team members and friends from the Nashville church helped us load our belongings into a moving truck for our move to Ohio. Our personal belongings had been significantly reduced by a very successful yard sale on the front lawn of the parsonage. Exhausted but excited, we said goodbye to our Brown County friends and headed to Chesapeake, Ohio, to begin our next most excellent adventure in ministry. It was May 24, 1974.

Upon arrival in Chesapeake, we unloaded our furniture and began making plans to remodel the downstairs of one of the two story houses to become our home. Brent was five years old and Sharianne was three. Chesapeake is located directly across the Ohio River from Huntington, West Virginia. The houses across the street from the ministry compound are built on the banks of the Ohio River. As we lay in bed at night, we could hear the peaceful sound of the tug boats churning up and down the river, pushing long barges of coal.

About twenty O.E. team members descended on this quiet little river town and began to rip houses apart to repurpose them for the ministry. As we were all fairly young and several sported long hair, rumors began to circulate that we were a bunch of hippies who had come to town to establish a commune. Until we finished our remodeling project, we did live somewhat communally, cooking and eating our meals together at the church next door. Those were fun times!

O.E. eventually had a dozen evangelistic teams traveling about the country, but in the early days, it was Dave and the Watchmen Quartet and Jenny Sue and I. A couple of other team members traveled doing promo for the ministry and there were a couple of ladies who did secretarial work. My first summer of travels was fully-booked with ministry in Christian camps and churches. Our Dodge van served as a home away from home for Jenny Sue, the kids, and I. We slept in our van when we served in Christian camps and camped in it as we traveled between engagements. After leading churches for several years, this was a much more relaxed style of ministry. Hey, it was the 70s! A lot of people were mobile, moving around the country. We felt like gypsies or hippies and loved it.

While we lived in Chesapeake, Ohio, I attended a branch campus of the University of Kentucky in Ashland, Kentucky, where I studied photography and dark room technology. After building a darkroom at the O.E. facility, I began doing much of the photography and darkroom work for the mission. I also taught some of the other O.E. team members to do the same. I loved the countless hours I spent in the darkroom developing film and enlarging photographs. To this day, I can go through the motions of loading 35 mm film into a film canister in the dark. The smell of vinegar still reminds me of the solutions I used to develop film and enlargements in the darkroom. The professor at the KU branch campus lost my final test, but gave me an A as my final grade. So, I can brag that I am a 4.0 student at the University of Kentucky. In those days I built my own dissolve unit for two Kodak slide projectors and shot and developed slides to create multi-media presentations to aid in my preaching. I also wrote and recorded music while we lived in Chesapeake. That was a very creative time in my life.

Jenny Sue and I spent eighteen years ministering with O.E. How do I put eighteen years of ministry all over the United States and to foreign countries into print? Well, I abbreviate. Following are some of those abbreviated stories.

AN EVENTFUL MEETING IN
WHITEWATER INDIANA

One of the first youth revivals I conducted with O.E. was at the Christian Church in Whitewater, Indiana, a small town just north of Richmond, Indiana. It was an enjoyable meeting with the youth and adults of the Whitewater church. I especially remember a teaching on the Sermon on the Mount I did with the youth group, sitting under a huge Oak tree in a public park. One of the youth paid special attention to the teaching. They called him Wayne, which was actually his middle name. Wayne, a freshman in high school and a very deep thinker, was interested in my ministry, so we spent time talking about ministry while I was in Whitewater. I also went to Wayne's high school to do an assembly. I did many high school assemblies in my years with O.E., which were a combination of singing with my guitar and stand-up Christian comedy. After the assembly, Wayne told me I had inspired him to become a Christian musician. I encouraged him to pursue his dream, but I wondered if one so young would stick with it.

After that, Wayne would occasionally attend meetings I held around the area. Once, Wayne and his mother came to North Vernon, Indiana and spent the weekend in a motel to attend a youth revival I was conducting. A few years later, I talked with Wayne when I was singing at the Jesus House in Cincinnati. He was a student at Cincinnati Bible College, where he was composing Christian music on piano. I once again encouraged him to pursue his dream.

Did Wayne stick with his dream to become a Christian musician? Wayne's full name was Richard Wayne Mullins. The world came to know him as Rich Mullins, one of the best Christian singer/song writer/musicians I have known. I am so honored that I was able to inspire Rich in his formative years, for he spent the rest of his life inspiring me with his music, his teachings, and his life lived on the ragged edge for Jesus. Rich Mullins was a consummate Jesus Freak!

When our son Brent was in high school, he attended a conference at a college in Illinois that offered a degree in Christian Music. Rich Mullins did a concert at that conference. When Rich discovered that Brent was in the audience, he had Brent stand. Rich encouraged the people to take Brent out to lunch, because Brent's dad (me) had been a big encouragement to him (Rich). Rich then recounted the story of my teaching on the Sermon on the Mount with his youth group. Rich told the audience that teaching had changed his life. I am humbled to see how my preaching and teaching has impacted so many lives through my many years in ministry. Thank you Jesus!

I was deeply grieved when I learned that Rich had been killed in a tragic automobile accident. I am sad there will never be another new Rich Mullins album, but I treasure the ones I have.

THAR AIN'T NONE!

In October of 1974, I drove from Chesapeake, Ohio to Tazewell, West Virginia to do an assembly at a high school. I got turned-around driving through the mountains, so I stopped at a service station to ask directions. A man working outside took one look at this long-haired young fellow getting out of a tricked-out van and didn't want anything to do with me. I greeted the man kindly and asked if he could please tell me how to get to Tazewell, West Virginia. He didn't even look up from his work, but sneered, "Thar ain't none"! I pointed to Tazewell on my map. That seemed to irritate the man even more than my appearance and he finally replied, "If you're lookin' for Taz'ell, I can tell you how to get thar". The locals dropped the W in Tazewell. How stupid of me not to know that!

When I arrived at the high school, there was a group of black kids standing out front. I introduced myself, asked if they would help carry my musical equipment, and they kindly obliged. I did not know that there was racial tension between the blacks and whites, because no blacks had been selected for the High School Homecoming Court. When the white kids saw the black kids carrying my musical equipment, they decided to not like me.

As I began my concert, a young white girl seated in front of the stage began to heckle me and continued with no one making any attempt to stop her. I finally stopped singing and said, "You're the weirdest person that I ever met. What planet are you from"? She shouted back, "I'm from Columbus, Indiana"! I said, "You're kidding, I used to live in Nashville, Indiana"! I asked if we could talk after the concert, so she settled down and I continued. As I concluded the concert with a comedy routine about falling in love in the first grade and an explanation of God's agape love, the students became very quiet. I knew the Holy Spirit was at work.

After the concert, many of the students thanked me for coming and for my music and words. A teacher asked if I would come to her class and explain this "agape love", stating that she said that she had never heard of it before. So, I was privileged to lecture to a classroom full of high school students about the four words for love in the Greek language and how agape was a special love that came from God. Wow!

When I finished speaking to the class, I returned to the auditorium to load my musical equipment in my van. The football coach was waiting for me and offered to help. After we had packed my equipment in my van, the coach said he needed to take some equipment over to the practice field and asked if I would ride along. We got in his car and, as he pulled away, the coach turned to me and said, "I used to know the Lord, but I've gotten away from Him. I now know that I need to get back. What do I need to do"? I was blessed to share Scripture with the coach and pray with him to recommit his life to Christ. Ministry doesn't get much better than that!

I could have never anticipated what happened at the high school in Tazewell, West Virginia. At the beginning, it looked like it might be a disaster, but God had a plan. He always does!

JESUS FREAK PREACHER

It was in those early years of ministry with O.E., that I was first called a "Jesus Freak". I think the people who called me that meant to be critical and I felt criticized. Then, I researched the meaning of freak and it totally changed my perspective on being called a Jesus Freak. A freak is "something conspicuously deviated from that which is normal". Since I met Jesus, there has been nothing normal about my life. It has been fantastic! After that, I began to wear the term Jesus Freak like a badge and thanked people for calling me that.

A Brush With Legalism

After the assembly at the high school in Tazewell, I drove to Bluefield, West Virginia to spend a couple of days with a buddy who taught at an area Christian college. Many of the staff members were very legalistic and didn't like Jesus Freaks like me. My friend invited me to sing and speak at the college chapel service. He warned me that some of the staff would probably hate me, but the students would love me. He wanted me to show the students a non-legalistic approach to living for Jesus. I felt like Daniel being thrown to the lions, but actually relished the challenge.

My friend and I drove to the college and spent the morning sharing with students and staff members before the late morning chapel service. I had met some of the students at a week of camp held on the grounds of the college. A well-known evangelist from the area happened to be at the college that day to attend the chapel service. I had heard that he was a very legalistic man. Seeing him standing outside the chapel, I went over to introduce myself. As I stuck out my hand to shake his, he stared at my hand, looked at my hair, and walked away. My friend remarked, "That's okay, he won't speak to anyone with hair over their ears". Expecting that kind of reception from the man, I wasn't ruffled. I was secure in my identity and no narrow-minded evangelist could threaten it. I actually felt sorry for the man.

As my friend had said, the students loved my ministry and some of the staff didn't. I drove away from the college feeling like I had accomplished exactly what Jesus had sent me there to do. Life was good!

MY OWN STRUGGLES
WITH LEGALISM

I would be remiss, if I didn't admit that I struggled with legalism in the early years of my ministry. Some of my instructors at OBC tended to be legalistic, but I don't blame them. Some of the young preachers that I hung around with were legalistic, but I don't blame them. I think the blame for my legalism lay solely within me. I was failing to obey Jesus' great commandment to love Him and love people with all my heart, soul, mind, and strength. That caused me to be exclusive and judgmental at times and caused me to make enemies of people who should have been my friends. The spiritual fervor of the Jesus Movement washed a lot of that legalism right out of me.

I vividly remember serving in a week of camp in 1969. I was carrying bitterness from my first fulltime ministry. As with many weeks of camp during the Jesus Movement, this week of camp turned into a revival. The Holy Spirit was moving powerfully one night during the vespers service. Young people were streaming to the front of the building to repent of their sins and receive prayer. Suddenly, I found myself included. I walked to the front of the building, got on my knees, and began weeping and repenting of my attitude. It was embarrassing, because I was one of the leaders of the week of camp. It was also very humbling, but I needed an experience with humility to deal with my pride. People gathered around me, laid hands on me, and prayed for me. It was exhilarating! A preacher friend, who was at that week of camp, said that he saw a big change in me from that day forward. Thank you Jesus!

THROWN TO THE LIONS ONCE AGAIN

I had another experience with legalism at a church in Ohio. A good friend invited me to do an assembly at a high school close to where he preached. He then asked me to do a similar concert at his church. Like my friend in West Virginia, he warned that some of the people would not like my concert, because they even thought John Denver's music was of the devil. Others in the church thought that it was sinful to play a guitar in a church service. My friend said he wanted me to show the younger folk an alternate approach to living for Jesus. Once again, I felt like Daniel being thrown to the lions, but I was up to the challenge.

I love the word "anoint" in the New Testament. It means "something that has oil smeared on it". Oil, in the New Testament, often refers to the work of the Holy Spirit. To be anointed is to be empowered by the Holy Spirit. I never feel more anointed by the Holy Spirit, than when I am ministering in a somewhat hostile environment. The Holy Spirit definitely anointed me as I did my concert. After the concert, as I was receiving hugs and words of appreciation, someone said, "Don, you wouldn't believe what that lady over there is saying about you". I asked who they were referring to and they pointed to an angry woman who was staring holes through me. I thought for a moment about how Jesus would respond and decided to meet her anger with love. I walked over to the woman, introduced myself, shook her hand, and told her how much I appreciated her being at the service. I said, "God bless you", but I did restrain from hugging her. I think she needed a hug as much as anyone I ever met.

WHERE GOD GUIDES HE PROVIDES

In October of 1974, Jenny Sue, the kids, and I traveled to Etowah, Tennessee for a weekend youth revival. On the way to Etowah I held a high school assembly in Clinton, Tennessee. Etowah is a beautiful little town located on the Hiwassee River in the Appalachian Mountains. We were there at the peak of fall color. It was beautiful! The weekend of meetings went very well; however, when we were ready to return home, the treasurer of the church informed me that funds were tight and they would not be able to pay me for the weekend. We did not have enough money to make it back to Chesapeake and, in that day, did not have a credit card. We prayed and believed that we should drive home, knowing that we did not have money for gas or food. We just trusted God to provide. Passing close to Lookout Mountain, we decided to stop. Besides, it was free. As we were exiting our van, a sizable amount of money blew across the parking lot. We gathered up the money and went inside the office to ask if anyone had reported lost money. The attendant said, "No, I guess it's yours". With that money, we were able to refill our gas tank and buy food on our trip home. Praise God!

During my traveling ministry, I often prayed for a specific amount of money to pay my bills or purchase new equipment for my ministry. On numerous occasions, as people passed me leaving a service, they would shake my hand and leave a monetary gift in my hand. I learned not to draw attention to their gift, just quietly slip the gift into my pocket, thank them, and let them know that God had used them to answer my prayers. Often, when I was able to pull the gift out of my pocket in a private place, I would find that it was the exact amount of money I needed. God is good and where He guides, He provides!

A Flurry of Ministry

Over the next several years, I conducted hundreds of high school assemblies, youth revivals, adult revivals, concerts, rallies, and retreats. I sang and spoke at dozens of Christian colleges and in hundreds of churches and weeks of camp. It was such a flurry of ministry activity that, even though I still have calendars from those years, I do not recall many of the events.

I do recall a youth revival I conducted in Vevay, Indiana, a beautiful town on the Ohio River. The pastor, a World War II veteran, had been injured in a plane crash during the war. He was a great guy. I still remember some of the stories he told about the war. Jenny Sue and I stayed in a cute little camper on the banks of the river. At the beginning of the weekend, I did a concert in a public park in downtown Vevay. I also remember going to a restaurant in town where teens hung out. After I finished eating with a leader of the church, I excused myself and went over to a table where some teens were sitting. Asking to join them, I sat down, introduced myself, and invited them to the youth revival. Gradually, most of the teens left, but one young lady, who seemed interested in talking, stayed. I shared the Gospel with her and was privileged to pray with her to receive Christ as her Savior. She came to the youth revival, made a public confession of Christ, and was baptized.

It's the Church!

As I said earlier, I ministered in a "bazillion" Christian camps during my traveling years. Two of my favorites were Camp Christian in Mill Run, Pennsylvania and Rainbow Camp (now called The Ark) in Converse, Indiana. I ministered in both camps every year for almost twenty years. I met hundreds of people who blessed my life immeasurably. If I could go back and redo all those weeks of camp, I would gladly do it! I know that is impossible, because I don't have the energy and I can't recreate the past. I do relive the memories and I feel very privileged to have made them.

A special week at Rainbow Camp is still vivid in my memory. My good friend Bill Roberts led worship and I preached during the evening worship service. Bill, an anointed worship leader, incorporated a teaching on the Tabernacle in his worship set. I preached from Second Corinthians on the section called The New Covenant. The Holy Spirit visited the worship service every night and many of the teens responded to the invitation to accept Jesus as Savior or renew faith in Him. One night a Youth Minister came forward to confess his sins and ask forgiveness. His youth group gathered around him, laid hands on him, and prayed for him. That night was very touching and very loud. The Camp Manager heard the noise, came over to investigate, and asked me what was going on. I said, "I think it's the Holy Spirit". He nodded agreement and left.

A lady, who was teaching one of the morning classes, told her students that she had a tumor and would see her doctor that afternoon to discuss treatment. She asked the teens to pray for her. The teens gathered around her, laid hands on her, and prayed for her healing. When she was examined by her doctor that afternoon, the tumor had disappeared. Praise the Lord!

The last event of the week was a huge bonfire on Friday night, before the camp dismissed on Saturday morning. That scene is permanently burned into my memory. About a hundred teens and half as many adults were gathered around the bonfire, weeping, hugging, and praying for one another. The group spontaneously went from one worship song to the next, with no one actually leading. The glow of the bonfire made people's faces look angelic. I was worshipping, with my hands lifted lost in the moment, when Bill elbowed me and asked, "Hey, Whetstine! Do you know what this is"? It took a moment to return to Planet Earth and respond to his question. I said, "No, what is it"? I hope I never forget his answer. He said, "It's The Church"! As I looked around the bonfire, I saw The Church in all its glory and simplicity. There was no building or fancy pews. There was no earthly person even leading what was happening, for the Holy Spirit was in control. I saw a group of people, madly in love with Jesus and one another, responding to the leading of His Spirit. That's The Church!

Vacation Evangelism

While ministering with O.E., Jenny Sue, the kids, and I vacationed several times in Florida around Christmas. We drove our camper van and camped near the beach, often in the Keys. One day, as I sat on the beach in Key West playing my guitar, a young man sat down beside me. He asked what kind of music I was into. I cut to the chase and said, "Jesus music"! He looked at me intensely and asked, "What does Jesus do for you"? I didn't give him any theology, just answered his question by sharing things that Jesus does for me. When I finished, the young man said, "That's heavy", walked out on a jetty, and sat looking out over the ocean. After a while he returned, sat down beside me and said, "Tell me some more". In the course of our conversation, he told me his story. He was a teacher from Michigan, who after teaching for several years, felt unfulfilled. So, he quit his job, sold his house and most of his belongings, and came to Key West. His goal was to buy a sail boat he could live on, find some friends he loved, and share life with them. I told him I believed that he was looking for love, joy, and peace. He agreed. I then read from Galatians chapter five and told him that God wanted to give him love, joy, and peace as the fruit of a relationship with Jesus. I was blessed to pray with him to receive Christ as Savior. I gave him a Bible and encouraged him to read it. He was sharing his new-found faith with other young people on the beach by the end of the week.

Delivered

My preacher friend, Bob, asked me to be part of a team to minister to a teen deeply involved in Satanism. He had been in trouble with the law and in and out of several mental health facilities. The team included the teen's Probation Officer, who insisted on being present. At the mention of God or Jesus, the teen would go berserk. Though he had been raised in the church, he could no longer attend, because it triggered violent episodes. Mental Health professionals found no basis for his unusual behavior and sent him home to his parents, who contacted my friend Bob.

The boy's parents invited us to their home to minister to their son. When we questioned him about his involvement in Satanism, he told us he was a High Priest in a Satanic Church and his responsibilities were to conduct orgies and animal sacrifices. As I read Scripture to the teen, he went berserk. Spit and mucous violently flew from his mouth and nose and hit the wall on the other side of the room. He thrashed about wildly until Bob demanded, "Stop your attack in the name of Jesus"! The teen immediately calmed and fell over on the couch in a semi-conscious state. An evil, guttural voice began to speak through the teen and said he was Satan, but Bob asked, "In the name of Jesus, is that true"? The voice said, "No"! We gathered around the teen, anointed him with oil, laid hands on him, and began to pray. He reacted violently and then passed-out, but we continued to pray. After a while, he calmly sat up and said, "I taste blood". I replied, "I think you have tasted blood, the blood of Jesus"! As we left the home that evening, the teen's Probation Officer confessed that he had never seen anything like that and almost wet his pants.

As I said previously, attending church triggered violent episodes with the teen. He was in church the following Sunday with his parents. I was also present and watched him worshipping from the depth of his soul, with a broad smile on his face. It was Easter Sunday! How fitting!

Ministering In Haiti

While working with O.E., I was blessed to make several ministry trips to foreign countries. One of the first was to Haiti. After reading a lot about Haiti, I was still unprepared for what I experienced when I arrived. Soldiers with submachine guns patrolled the airport, scrutinizing everything we carried. A member of our group said, if one of the soldiers decided to take my expensive camera, I should just let him have it. Our group loaded into the back of a truck with an open top and drove three hours along the coast, up into the mountains to Dessalines. It was January and below zero in Indiana and only twenty-four degrees in Miami. When we arrived in Haiti, it was eighty degrees and very sunny. After the three hour trip in an open truck, we were all sunburned. On the trip to Dessalines I took lots of pictures, because I had never seen such poverty and wanted to record it. I also saw a lot of beauty in that island nation.

We were in Haiti to work with Brother Duhon, a veteran missionary from a French-speaking background in Louisiana. He closed his ministry of church planting when he was sixty-five and flew to Haiti to begin a new ministry. He began preaching on the streets of Porte Prince, where he rented a car and slept in it. Later, he bought a box truck and lived in it. Eventually, he migrated to Dessalines, where he baptized hundreds of people, trained dozens of preachers, and built many church buildings in just a few years. Brother Duhon was an amazing man! We were there to help finish the construction of a training center and do evangelistic work in the surrounding villages.

Brother Duhon warned us not to eat or drink anything that had not been canned or bottled. Potatoes were safe if they were peeled and thoroughly cooked, as were onions. We ate a lot of Spam and potatoes while we were in Haiti. With a slice of onion and hot sauce, Spam isn't that bad! Brother Duhon also warned that, if we touched a Haitian, we should wash and disinfect our hands before we ate. It was hard not to touch Haitians, for they were very friendly and would sometimes walk up and hold your hand as you walked down the street. Even though Brother Duhon warned us to take care, he ate the local food, drank the water, and was never sick. That had to be God's supernatural protection.

A few of us stayed with the missionary in his home, where I was befriended by a cute little Haitian girl, about eight years old. I remember her rubbing my hand to see if the white would come off. She would sit with me on the missionary's porch, hold my hand, and talk non-stop. How I wish I could have understood her, but I did not speak Creole. Brother Duhon said that she was an orphan and lived with whoever took her in and fed her. I asked if I might be able to adopt her and he said it would be virtually impossible. I am tearing-up as I think of her all these years later. If I could have smuggled her out of the country, I would have gladly done so. I often wonder what her life is like today, or if she is even alive.

I spent a day with a nurse who worked with the mission. She had a clinic in her home, where she dealt with every manner of disease or injury imaginable. I watched her stitch a cut using Cloraseptic to numb the wound. Every morning, when she opened her gate, a long line of people would be waiting for medical treatment. She treated them from dawn 'til dark. The day I was there, a lady had walked several hours over the mountains to bring her small baby to be treated. When she arrived, her beautiful baby, not much larger than a Barbee Doll, had died. When the nurse was not busy at her clinic, she rode a donkey to neighboring villages to treat people. I only spent one day with that remarkable servant of Jesus. One day in her world was all I could emotionally endure.

During the day, our group worked on the training center. In the evenings, we traveled to neighboring villages to hold evangelistic meetings. I loved traveling to the meetings with the Haitian Christians, who sang all the way there and back. The more excited they became, the louder and higher they sang. Their beautiful dark chestnut brown skin made them invisible at night, until they smiled. Their big bright smiles lit-up the night.

On one such trip, we traveled to one of the poorest areas in Haiti to minister in a church building made of bamboo poles covered with palm fronds. A Typhoid Quarantine sign was posted on the building. We were told not to worry, because we were taking Typhoid meds. The little building was packed. I sat near the front next to a Haitian woman with two sets of twins. Three of her children had orange hair, which meant they had no protein in their bodies. One of her babies lay in the crook of her arm staring up at me. I tried to get the baby's attention, but its eyes were fixed, because it was near brain dead from malnutrition. Shortly thereafter, I am sure several of her babies died, she wrapped them in palm leaves, and buried them in her backyard. When worship began, this lady came alive. She danced, shouted, and smiled the biggest smile imaginable! I stood next to her thinking, "I came to Haiti to tell this woman something"?! She needed to teach me! When I got back to the states, I could not get that woman off my mind. As I recounted the story to a friend, he put it in perspective. He said, "When Jesus is the only thing you have, you are truly wealthy". That woman may have been one of the wealthiest persons I ever met.

MINISTERING IN THE
DOMINICAN REPUBLIC

Another memorable trip was to the Dominican Republic. My friend Russ, whom I met in a camp in Pennsylvania, was the director of a Christian school for teens from all over the world. The school, Escuela Caribe, was located in Jarabacoa, several hours up into the mountains from Santo Domingo. On the spectacular drive to the school, we passed a mansion built by the son of Christopher Columbus. The mountains were covered with palm trees, hardwood trees, pine trees, and many types of flowering shrubs. The ground was covered with a thick carpet of bent grass, like you see on golf greens here in the states.

Russ invited me to the D.R. to lead worship and preach at a retreat for the teens from Escuela Caribe. Many of the teens, from wealthy families who could no longer control them, were court-ordered to the school to experience some culture shock and Christian discipline. Russ, his wife, and a group of staff members from the school, oversaw the retreat held at a nearby camp. I was offered a bunk with the staff, but I elected to sleep in the boy's dormitory to get better acquainted with the boys. I didn't sleep much, for this was a group of very troubled teenagers who had night terrors and sleep-walked. I awoke one night to find a teenage boy leaning over my bunk staring at me. I lay awake and prayed a lot that week.

A behavioral modification system was practiced at the school. The teens earned privileges by practicing better behavior. Lowest ranking students wore jail uniforms and flip flops, while higher ranking students dressed normally. Low ranking students were required to be with an adult staff member at all times and ask permission to go to the bathroom, accompanied by a staff member. It was obvious that good behavior mattered and I was amazed at how well the system was working.

The first time I led worship, spiritual conflicts erupted. Some of the students had been involved in witchcraft or cults, others struggled with addiction. During worship, some of the students would freak-out and the counselors would take them out to console them.

Jenny, a cute sixteen-year-old girl from New York, would not let me near her. Like my wife Jenny Sue, she had blond hair and blue eyes, but behind her pretty blue eyes lurked something dark and evil. One day, while Jenny sat alone at the lunch table, I walked up behind her, embraced her in a bear hug, and said, "Jenny, Jesus loves you and I do too". She began to weep, looked up at me and said, "Don, I need help". Russ, his wife, and I took Jenny outside to minister to her. We asked if we could pray for her and she consented. As we laid hands on her and began to pray, she fell to the ground, screamed, and threw up. Kneeling beside her, we continued to pray. Jenny puked until she could puke no more, then began to dry heave. Finally, she calmed a little and Russ's wife asked, "Jenny, can you say Jesus is Lord"? She tried her best, but could not say those words and began to hyperventilate from the effort. She paused and then, with great effort, said,

"J-J-J- Jesus"! I had my hand on her back and felt her immediately relax. With a broad smile, Jenny sat up and loudly declared, "Jesus is Lord"!

I was also blessed to minister to a Jewish girl named Daphne, an Israeli citizen born in Jerusalem. Interested in my last name, she asked if I was Jewish. I told her I had Jewish ancestors. I asked Daphne if she realized that Jesus was Jewish. She said, "No way"! Somehow, she had never considered the fact that Jesus was actually Jewish. Daphne did not accept the New Testament, so I began to talk with her about the Messianic prophecies in the Old Testament, pointing out how Jesus had fulfilled all of them. One day, she told me that she wanted to accept Jesus Christ as her Messiah. This poor boy, who grew up in the north end of Franklin, Indiana, got to pray with a Jewish girl, who grew up in Jerusalem, to receive Jesus as her Messiah. It doesn't get much better than that! Sadly, the next day, Daphne's brother Will, also a student at Escuela Caribe, told Daphne she was dead to him and he would never acknowledge her again. A few months later, my friends from the school informed me that Will had given his life to Christ. Whoohoo!

MINISTRY IN THE FROZEN NORTH

I made an eventful trip to Canada to minister in a retreat for teens, held at a camp in Central Ontario. You did notice that I said camp? It was February and I don't think I have ever been colder! You know? That kind of cold that freezes your nose hairs as you breathe! I saw the Northern Lights like I have never seen them in the lower forty-eight. It was incredible! God was really showing-off!

The teens attending the retreat were from the Christian Churches and a group of churches that traced their roots to Christian reformer Abner Jones, who was active in New England in the early 1800s. I especially enjoyed talking with the teens and youth leaders from the Abner Jones heritage. Their beliefs were very fundamental, but they had some interesting perspectives on the Christian faith. Eighteen years of traveling ministry, in many denominations and independent churches, has given me an appreciation for the diverse nature of the Body of Christ.

Spiritually, there wasn't much happening in the Canadian churches in those days. I sensed a spiritual vacuum and hunger in the people that the Holy Spirit loves to fill. Jesus said that those who hunger and thirst after righteousness get filled. As I led worship, teens and adults participated with all their hearts. As I preached, I watched people being enlightened and touched by the Word. There were many responses to invitations to renew commitment to Jesus. I prayed with and counseled people late into the night. It was one of those times I knew that I was in the exact place I should be, doing exactly what God led me to do. I preached Jesus, and loved His people.

At the conclusion of the retreat, I traveled back to Toronto, where I ministered in a couple of churches. After being in dirty U.S. cities, I was impressed with the cleanness of Toronto. I was also aware that ministry in Toronto was very different than in U.S. cities. Most of the people lived in apartment buildings and you needed permission to enter the building. Churches were actually planting members in different apartment complexes to reach people for the Lord. It was an enlightening and fruitful time of ministry in the frozen north.

On my way back from Canada, I flew into Buffalo, where the plane landed in a blizzard. I envisioned spending a couple of days stranded in the Buffalo airport, but I was able to take one of the last flights out before they closed the airport. Thank you Jesus!

ICCH

One of the joys of my traveling years was my association with the Indiana Children's Christian Home. As the name implies, the home was located in Indiana and existed to minister to troubled Indiana children, who ranged in age from about ten years to late teens. Most of the children at ICCH were court-ordered to the facility, because they had been declared incorrigible and had been in trouble with the law. I was really impressed with the educators, counselors, and administrators who served with ICCH—they were dedicated, professional, good people. My primary association with the home was to serve in a week of camp held yearly at various Christian camps. I led worship and preached at weeks of camp with ICCH for about fifteen years, where I was punched, kicked, bitten, cussed, and hugged by the kids. I loved all of it! As the ICCH staff became more acquainted with me, they released me to do spiritual counseling with the children and I was able to pray with many to commit their lives to Christ. I was also privileged to minister to many of the ICCH staff. God knows how much the staff needed spiritual encouragement, they had a hard job!

I heard heart-breaking stories about the dysfunctional homes from which these kids came. I remember a young boy, who had been transported to ICCH by two Deputy Sheriff's, who shackled his hands and feet to get him in and out of their vehicle. They carried him into a counselor's office, kicking, cussing, and spitting, where they zip-tied him to a chair and left, wishing the counselor good luck. When I met him, he had become a very sweet responsible kid through the ministry of ICCH.

I also remember another amazing young boy, who came to the home at age ten, after murdering one of his prostitute sister's lovers. The boy slept on the couch in his dysfunctional home and, one night, became enraged when he wanted to go to sleep, but his sister was using the couch to have sex with one of her clients. The man swore at the boy, who went to the closet, came back with a shotgun, and blew him away. How do you prosecute a ten-year-old boy for murder? That was the dilemma faced by the court, who ordered the boy to ICCH. I said earlier that the boy was amazing and I was amazed at his resiliency to work through his horrid past and become the amazing kid I met.

Through the years, I made many trips to the ICCH facility to minister in their chapel service or just hang out with the children and staff. Unfortunately, ICCH no longer exists, because the government withdrew funding from faith-based facilities like theirs. But, the memories exist and I keep them stored in a special place in my heart!

LOVIN' ME SOME MEXICO

I made numerous trips to Mexico in the years I traveled with O.E., but it would take volumes to record all my experiences. Let it suffice to say that I love Mexico, ministering in Mexico, the Mexican people, and real Mexican food. On a trip with a group of O.E. team members, we once ate at The Oasis, a Mexican Restaurant between Tijuana and Tecate. We knew there was a good chance we would be sick, but we ate the food anyway, because it was so good. I also remember eating Jalapeños in a restaurant in San Louis Potosi. A Mexican man gave me some good advice. He said, "Hey Gringo! Don't let them touch your lips". Once, when bartering with a shopkeeper in a market in Satillo, I said, "No gracias" and walked away. The shopkeeper wanted to call me back and offer me a better price, but he did not know what to call me. He shouted, "Hey, Ronald Reagan"! I guess that was about as American as he could imagine. And, I will never forget a cute little girl name Rosa, whom I met at an orphanage in Queretaro. She was named Rosa, because a missionary watched a family, unable to take care of her, place her in the middle of a street in Rosa and drive away.

LIVING IN THE WRONG STATE

I loved living at the ministry compound and working with the other team members, but I felt like I was living in the wrong state. I would travel to Indiana to minister, then travel back to Ohio, only to return to Indiana the following week. I was not centrally located for the ministry I was doing. Plus, Jenny Sue and I wanted to live closer to our families in Indiana. We began to pray that God would open a door for us to move back to Indiana. As we prayed, a plan visualized. We believed that God would move us back to Indiana to build a house of our own where we would open the first Regional Office of Operation Evangelize. We also felt this would happen in about a year. We shared our plan with the O.E. leadership, but they appeared skeptical.

While we were praying, we were contacted by a couple who had been members of the church in Nashville. They asked us to meet them at the parking lot of the IGA Grocery Store in Beanblossom, Indiana. We drove to Beanblossom and met our friends, with no clue what the meeting was about. When we arrived, our friends were waiting for us. They jumped in our van and said, "Let's take a ride". They directed us to drive west on SR 45 and turn onto Morrison Road, where they had once lived and still owned property. We drove up the road about a half mile and our friends said, "Stop"! The man got out of our van and began searching for a survey stake. When he found it, he said, "Let's take a walk in the woods". It was February, it was cold, and spitting snow. After we had walked a hundred feet or so into the woods, my friend said, "Do you like this place"? I said, "Yes, it's beautiful". My friend replied, "Then it's yours, God said to give it to you". Wow! This couple knew that we wanted to relocate to Indiana and, while praying for us, the Lord told the man to give us property in Brown County. He went to his wife and asked her to continue praying for us and tell him what the Lord said. Eventually, she told her husband that she believed the Lord wanted them to give us property in Brown County. That was the confirmation the man needed before he contacted us. In answer to our prayers to relocate to Indiana, the Lord moved a couple of friends to give us three and a half acres of property in Brown County. Once again, as we sought God's direction, He opened a door big enough to drive a Mack truck through.

We now had property to build our house, but we didn't have money to build it. I didn't need a lot of money, because we planned to build the house ourselves. I met with officials at banks around Nashville asking to borrow money, but in 1978 money was tight and banks did not want to loan money for construction with only property as collateral.

A group of ladies from the Christian Church in Nashville, on their way to a Bible study, were discussing our difficulty borrowing money to build our house. One of the ladies in the car said, "Well, they should contact me. I could loan them the money". She was a retired school teacher and I didn't even think she liked me when I was her Pastor five years earlier. In fact, we had a couple of retired teachers in the congregation who often pointed out their dislike for my use of slang or corrected my grammar. I met with the lady and she loaned us the money to build our house. Wow! Someone gave us property in answer to our prayers and a lady who didn't seem to like me when

I was her Pastor, loaned us the money to build our house. You can't make stuff like that up!

Almost exactly a year after I informed the leadership of O.E. that we would be moving to Indiana in a year, we were packing a moving van to move to Indiana. God is so good!

Mud, Horse Flies, and Building Woes

We arrived in Indiana full of excitement about this new phase of our lives. Once our house was livable, we would be back in Brown County, living the dream in the place we felt like we belonged. In the meantime, we lived with Jenny Sue's parents in the country near Franklin and stored our furniture in an outbuilding on the property.

When we started our house in June of 1979, I took a month off from traveling to work on the house. We hired a man that the locals called "Wild Bill" to do the excavation. Yep, he was wild! We poured the footers in a thunderstorm. I called the concrete company to ask them to cancel the delivery, but they said, "Sorry, the truck is on the way". That was a bad day with more to come. The remnants of two hurricanes passed through Indiana that spring and dumped twelve inches of rain on our building site. We constantly fought mud. One day, Jenny Sue and I were stuck in the mud almost to our knees, trying to dig the mud off the footers to begin laying the concrete blocks. We had one of the biggest, loudest fights of our entire marriage. If your marriage can survive building a house together, it can probably survive most anything.

I laid the concrete blocks while Jenny Sue carried blocks and mixed mortar. The house, built into a hill, had a walk-out on the lower back level. The front wall, built against the hill, required ten inch concrete blocks, while the side walls required eight inch blocks. A ten inch concrete block is very heavy, so my brother-in-law graciously volunteered to lay them. His eyes were so bloodshot at the end of the day that my sister thought he had been drinking. It seemed like every time I leaned over to lay a block, a horse fly bit me in the middle of my back. They were terrible that year, as were the deer flies. Between horse flies, mud, and dirt caving in on our footers, it was a frustrating start to building our dream home.

We moved into our house when it was barely livable and continued to finish it over the next year. Work slowed considerably when I was busy traveling. When I was on the road, Jenny Sue purchased building materials and had them on site when I returned home. Drywall dust and saw dust were everywhere in our house. We slept in it, ate it, and breathed it. Our daughter, Sharianne, actually liked our house before we hung the drywall. She bought a pair of clamp-on roller skates with a skate key at a yard sale for a quarter. With a bare concrete floor and open walls, she could skate through the entire lower level of our house. She had her own private roller rink. Sharianne lost the skates, but still has the key.

THE BEANBLOSSOM HOBBY FARM

O ne of our goals when settling on our homestead in the woods was to live a more self-sufficient lifestyle. Self-sufficiency was the rage in the 70s and I read Organic Gardening and Mother Earth News faithfully. I also wanted to emulate my Brown County ancestors who lived self-sufficiently on their homesteads. And, I still have some hippie DNA in me. Whatever the reasons, we were very content living our self-sufficient lifestyle on the place we dubbed The Beanblossom Hobby Farm. We eventually used the equity in our house to buy ten and a half adjoining acres, so the Hobby Farm now has fourteen acres.

Following are the lyrics to "Beanblossom Redneck", a song that I wrote to chronicle our history on the Beanblossom Hobby Farm:

(Chorus) I'm a Beanblossom Redneck, in the place where I belong and there's no finer place I'd rather be. You can have your city livin', I'll just keep my country ways. Livin' the dream in the place where I belong, just livin' the dream in the hills that I call home.

(Verse 1) If you drive the Bill Monroe Highway, you'll find our little town, known for Bluegrass Music all around. Stop at Brownie's Restaurant and sit and chat awhile, where biscuits, gravy, and coffee are always in style. Drive on down the highway and turn on that twisty road, up Rattlesnake Ridge to the place where we abode. You'll find our country homestead, with a whole lot of charm. It's the place we call the Beanblossom Hobby Farm.

(Verse 2) Well we don't have a poodle, a pug, or a fancy cat and I think it's fine if you're into that, but we've got a flock of chickens livin' in our coop. Our pets poop breakfast, yours just poop. Well we don't shop at Macy's or at some fancy mall. Rural King is our boutique and they've got it all. And beautiful downtown Beanblossom, may just have a mall. We call it Dollar General, that's all.

(Verse 3) We're doin' what we love most, through the Father, Son, and the Holy Ghost and we praise His name forevermore. He brought us to our place, as a working of His grace. How could we, ever want for more.

Beanblossom Redneck by Don Whetstine
2022 ARR UBP

After returning to Indiana, I continued to travel with O.E. for another thirteen years. Those were good years. I am grateful to God for the ministry He enabled me to do.

Restless Spirit

By 1992, eighteen years on the road had taken its toll. I was tired physically, mentally, and emotionally. Plus, I was about to turn fifty. My spirit was restless and I had this nagging feeling that I should be doing something else. One night, I awoke with my mind racing and sat at my computer typing my thoughts as quickly as they came. When I read what I had written, it was goals for future ministry, which could not include a traveling ministry. My heart was yearning for long-term relationships in ministry. I began to pray that God would open a door for that kind of ministry.

In the fall, I was returning from a Christian camp in Illinois, where I had conducted a retreat with a group of young adults. I was so tired from a busy summer of travels, I felt like I could have been declared legally dead. I was homesick, so I left as soon as the retreat was over and drove late into the night to get home. As I was driving, I whispered a prayer. I said, "Lord, this would be a good time to quit doing this". I arrived home in the early hours of the morning and, before I got out of bed, the Youth Minister from Franklin Memorial called. He said that Franklin Memorial wanted to add a new staff member and he thought I would be perfect for the job. They wanted someone to oversee small groups and ministry teams and also develop a contemporary worship service led by a praise band. He asked if I would be interested and I immediately said, "Yes"! Once again, in answer to my prayer for direction, God had opened a door big enough to drive a Mack truck through. And, He did it very quickly!

Loving Ministry in one Place

As I said earlier, I was longing to minister in one place and have long term relationships with people. I was also looking for a different style of church, for the Jesus Movement had forever stretched my wineskin. As I said earlier, I ministered in many different denominations and independent churches during my traveling years and grew to appreciate the diverse nature of the Body of Christ. I found brothers and sisters who were chest-deep in spiritual areas where I was just wading. I was especially drawn to churches that put more emphasis on the Holy Spirit, but I did not fit the typical Pentecostal or Charismatic models. Through the years, I have often been branded a Charismatic, but I never fully embraced that movement. I was more attracted to what Peter Wagner called the "Third Wave", which was his description of what the Holy Spirit was doing in the 80s and 90s. The Third Wave was neither Pentecostal (1st wave) nor Charismatic (2nd wave). When I left O.E., I hoped to either plant a Third Wave church or minister in one that already existed. That was probably the one thing that made me hesitant to accept a staff position with the Franklin Memorial Christian Church. I met with the other staff members and was pleased to find that they were in a similar place spiritually. We were kindred spirits!

I accepted the invitation to be on the pastoral staff and was hired by the leadership to become the Involvement Minister. I oversaw small groups and ministry teams and trained their leaders. I also helped develop a Contemporary Worship Service led by a praise band, with an emphasis on renewal.

This was a good fit for me, for I already had a long history with the church and many of the members were friends and relatives. My mom and dad were members of the church, along with my sister Jane and her husband. Cousins and high school classmates were members. This was the church where I was baptized, committed my life to the ministry, and that sponsored Jenny Sue and I to attend OBC. It was where I was ordained to the ministry, Jenny Sue and I were married, and the church supported my ministry during the years I traveled with O.E. For the first time in eighteen years, I was ministering in one place and I loved it!

DIGGING IN

I began bringing together a praise band that I led with my guitar. I found a lead guitar player, who recruited a friend to play drums. A teenager in the church owned a bass guitar, but could barely play. I offered to teach her to play and the use of my bass amp, if she would agree to play with the praise band. She agreed and became our bass player. I also recruited singers, which included Jenny Sue. The praise team was coming together, but we needed a keyboard player. I asked a lady in the church, who played very well and owned an electronic keyboard, if she would play with the praise band. She said she got very nervous when she played publically and would probably have diarrhea. I told her I would pray hard for her not to get diarrhea, if she would give it a try. The first Sunday the praise band led worship for the contemporary service, she played and was fine. After we finished our worship set, I heard her loudly proclaim, "I didn't get diarrhea"!

The contemporary worship service took off like a brush fire and attracted many new people to the church. In 1992, contemporary worship was a new thing in the Christian Churches in our area, so we felt like we were on the cutting edge. People who attended the service were being saved regularly. It was awesome to see people with hands raised, eyes closed, lost in intimate worship. The attendance at the church ran about five-hundred per Sunday, but the leadership wanted to see the attendance increase to one-thousand. With so many people attracted by the contemporary service, it appeared that we were well on our way to meeting that goal.

It seemed a good option to offer a traditional service and a contemporary service, because the church members could choose the style of worship they preferred. The traditional service was led by a choir wearing robes and singing from hymnals. When the contemporary service outgrew the traditional service, the traditional people viewed the contemporary service as a threat.

SMALL GROUPS MEETING BIG NEEDS

I have long been a proponent of Small Groups, because they are a great way to meet the spiritual and emotional needs of the members of a church. A lot of ministry happened in the small groups we developed at Franklin Memorial. People found the anonymity they needed to open-up and talk about their spiritual struggles. It was rewarding to watch group members listen sympathetically to someone's story, offer words of encouragement, and then pray fervently for their needs. A recovering alcoholic, who attended the church, started a recovery group that was very successful. Jenny Sue and I led a codependency group that brought emotional healing to many of its members.

Tragedy struck a family who were part of one of our small groups. The husband, an excavator, was killed in a cave-in while working at a construction site. He had only been a Christian six months, but had grown significantly through his interaction with his small group. None of the ministry staff could be reached at the time of the accident. When we were finally notified and got to the home of the grieving family, their small group was there and had everything under control. In the coming days and weeks, that small group emotionally carried that family through their grief.

THE DOOR IS OPEN

I loved my office at Franklin Memorial. The door was usually open, unless I was involved in a counseling situation. I loved to have people drop by. Many just wanted to chat, so I made time for them. If I was not in my office, one friend would drop by and leave her "calling card"—books turned backwards on my shelves. I always knew that Tina had been there. After the loneliness I often experienced in my years on the road, I loved the constant interaction with people. Others came to ask questions, so I became "Don, the answer man". I did a lot of counseling and one-on-one discipleship in my office, and often had serious prayer times with people. On my 50th birthday, I arrived at the church to find a large yard sign announcing my birthday. I unlocked my office to find it full of black streamers and black balloons. I laughed a lot that day. Life was good at Franklin Memorial and I thought I just might stay there until I retired.

TEAMWORK WITH STAFF AND ELDERS

I especially enjoyed working with the staff members and elders at Franklin Memorial. We worked well together, because our ministry gifts complimented one another. The staff ate lunch together almost every day. Those were good times of fellowship. One spring, a local restaurant offered an all-you-can-eat special on King Crab Legs. When the Senior Minister, the Youth Minister, and I heard about it, we were on it! We ate lunch there for several days and devoured volumes of crab legs. After noticing the manager staring at us disapprovingly, we did not return. It's a good memory that I sure enjoyed making.

The Youth Minister organized a mission trip every year for teens in the church. I was blessed to be one of the adults included and I enjoyed those trips immensely. We took several trips to Mexico and two trips to Arizona to minister to Native Americans. I was usually included in weeks of camp and other outings with the teens.

New Purpose for an old Sanctuary

Franklin Memorial built a new sanctuary a few years before I joined the staff, so the old sanctuary was virtually unused. At one of our staff brainstorming sessions, we decided to turn the old sanctuary into a gymnasium. Members of the congregation, including myself, jumped to the task and completed the work quickly. Soon we had a great place to play basketball and volleyball. Volleyball teams were formed and, several nights of the week, the formerly unused sanctuary was once again filled with life. The volleyball league attracted several young couples to our church. We called it "side door evangelism"—people were attracted to our volleyball league and then became part of our church. Some of the traditional members of the church, who disliked the contemporary service, viewed the conversion of the old sanctuary into a gymnasium as the last straw. One of the more vocal dissenters said, "We've got a rock band at one end of the church and a gymnasium at the other"! It didn't seem to matter that people were being saved!

Goodbye Home Church

We began to notice small groups of people talking intently in the foyer before worship, passing around a sheet of paper, which people were signing. We soon learned that it was a petition to have the Senior Minister and I fired. I have joked through the years that I left Franklin Memorial because I had a sign from God—it had 125 signatures on it. One church member, whom I had known most of my life said, "I signed that petition, but it wasn't personal. I hope we can remain friends and you and Jenny Sue will come over for supper sometime". That is laughable! Sometimes you just have to laugh, for it will prevent you from becoming bitter, or crying. Besides, the Bible says that God laughs at the plans of men, so why can't I?

The elders of the church supported the staff, but all the authority in a church does not necessarily reside in the leadership. The wealthy, influential, lifelong members of a church also have a lot of authority. Soon, dissenters began to vote against un-liked changes by withholding their offerings. Even though the elders supported the direction of the church, we often felt like we were fighting for everything we accomplished. When the church fights, no one wins! Paul told the Corinthians, when they took sides, they were already defeated. I would be remiss if I did not say that personalities played a big part in the conflict and, under pressure, my attitude sometimes stunk.

One day, the Senior Minister had a meeting with the elders and, after the meeting, he informed the other staff members that he had resigned as Senior Minister of the church and had also offered the resignations of the Administrative Secretary, the Youth Minister, and I. A fifth staff member, the Music Director, who directed the choir and led worship at the traditional service, remained with the church. He and the choir members had a party to celebrate our resignations. What a fellowship! What a joy Divine! Leaning on the everlasting arms! Groan!

I soon forgave everyone involved in the conflict. I can honestly say that I have no animosity toward anyone in that church and am still friends with many of them. Ironically, a few years later the church implemented the very things for which we were forced out.

KICKED OUT OR CALLED OUT

I did not have a clue what I was going to do when we were forced out of Franklin Memorial. About a hundred and fifty people, most of whom were part of the contemporary worship service, also left the church. That included several of the elders, the praise band, and some of the small group leaders. Most of the teens also left the church. This group contacted the four former staff members and asked if we would continue to shepherd them by planting a church. We prayed together and felt like the Lord's blessing was on this proposal. Christ Fellowship Church was formed and the four former staff members from Franklin Memorial were once again shepherding a familiar flock. I began to think that, rather than being kicked out of Franklin Memorial, we were actually called out. It was good!

Christ Fellowship was not a program-driven church. We were a relationship-driven church. Our motto was: "Building Relationships That Last For Eternity". The church, open to the filling, empowering work of the Holy Spirit, began to depend on Him for guidance—to pray and wait for His direction. I thrived in this new church!

Shortly after Christ Fellowship began, the Senior Pastor asked the three other staff members for a five year commitment to the church. I told him I could not commit to five years, because I felt like I would only be there three years and leave to plant another church. Where did that come from?! It came from my "knower"—something that I know that I know in my knower and there is no way that I could have known it, if God had not downloaded it in my spirit. The Senior Pastor was unhappy with my position, but three years later, Christ Fellowship sent me out to plant New Covenant Fellowship. God is faithful!

HEARING GOD

In those days, I became more aware of God's voice in my spirit and began to depend more on His direction. Through the years, I have learned that God's voice is seldom audible, which seems like an oxymoron. God seldom speaks to us audibly, because we are connected to God spirit to spirit. The only time God may have spoken to me audibly, was the time that I fell asleep while driving and was awakened by someone shouting my name, which I mentioned earlier in the book. Romans 8:16 says, "The Spirit himself testifies with our spirit that we are God's children". When God desires to speak to us, He speaks in our spirit. His message can then become words in our head, a phrase in our inner dialogue, feelings, or something that you just know is true. I totally believe that God still uses the gifts of prophesy, word of knowledge, word of wisdom, and discernment to communicate with His people. When someone tells me they don't believe that God still speaks to people, I just assume they have not learned to discern God's voice in their spirit. I have also had dreams and visions that gave amazing direction to my ministry. I'll mention them later. As I have already stated in this book, I am not a Pentecostal, or a Charismatic. Someone once called me an "Empowered Fundamentalist". I'm okay with that, but I would rather think that I am just a Jesus Freak! I was recently talking with a retired pastor at Sam's Club. When he learned that I was also a retired pastor, he asked "what denomination I belonged to". I told him that I did not belong to a denomination. I was just a Jesus Freak. He nodded approval. I have never been a member of a denominational church. In fact, for thirty years, I have not even been part of a church that has formal membership and I have found it refreshing. I am a Fringe Radical, one who never quite buys into the system. Systems are usually changed by Fringe Radicals, not by people who totally commit to the system. I would like to think that Jesus, John the Baptist, and the Prophets were Fringe Radicals.

One day, during communion at Christ Fellowship, I noticed a lady sitting next to me, bent over praying intently. Suddenly, a phrase went through my head, "Jesus receives your anger". I was puzzled by this phrase and I began to wonder if I was angry with someone. Then, I knew in my "knower" that the message was not for me, it was for the lady sitting next to me. I did not want to speak this, because it sounded weird and I could be wrong! Conviction grew and I finally put my hand on her back, leaned over, and whispered in her ear, "Jesus receives your anger". I will never forget her reaction. She gasped, sat up, turned to me with her mouth wide-open, and said, "That's exactly what I was praying about"! I don't know what you would call that, but it sure looks like a word of knowledge to me.

Camaraderie in Ministry

At first, Christ Fellowship was a portable church. We bought an old house in Whiteland, where our offices were located, but worshipped in the gymnasium of an elementary school in Franklin. I loved those portable days. It was a lot of work to set-up and tear-down for worship each Sunday, but it was great camaraderie. We had fun and felt a lot of joy working together. Most of our praise band followed us to Christ Fellowship and I was regularly recruiting and training new worship leaders and team members. I loved ministering with the worship team. They were awesome people!

We eventually bought an old church building in Whiteland that had belonged to the Presbyterians. It was a bit formal for our tastes, so we began remodeling it to suit our rowdy, non-formal congregation. We pulled out the large pulpit, lectern, and choir rail, which opened the stage for our praise band. We began opening a set of double doors near the stage when our praise team practiced and neighbors sat in lawn chairs to listen. It was obvious there was a more lively church occupying the old Presbyterian building. We also took out the pews and replaced them with more comfortable padded stackable chairs. Soon we had to push out the back wall of the worship area, because the attendance had grown to four-hundred. The building had a full basement, which we used for fellowship meals and children's church. There was also a two story addition to the building, which provided classrooms and office space for our four staff members. Once again, I had an office that I really liked and people constantly dropped by. Tina soon began leaving her "calling card"—books turned backwards on my shelves. Life was good at Christ Fellowship and I felt like I was living the dream.

RESCUED FROM THE ENEMY

During my time as a pastor of Christ Fellowship, I became very involved in pastoral counseling. Our church attracted many wounded people, which we called "EGRs"—extra grace required. I was very thankful for the ministry assistants I had trained, who helped me minister to these people.

A lady whom I had not heard from in years called one day. I met her at a church in southern Indiana when she was a teenager and kept in touch with her through her college years, but lost contact with her thereafter. She was very distraught and wanted to talk, but was hesitant to share details over the phone. I asked her to come to Christ Fellowship the next Sunday and allow us to pray for her. She hesitantly agreed, but I really doubted that she would show. She did come, but was literally wringing her hands during the service and I expected her to bolt at any moment. She made it through the service and came forward at the conclusion of the service to receive prayer. I motioned for a ministry assistant to help. I asked the lady how I could pray for her and she said, "I can't tell you"! Suddenly, I knew what her problem was, because the Lord had whispered it in my spirit. I looked at her and said, "You're a lesbian, aren't you"? She freaked-out and shouted, "There is no way that you could have known that"! I responded, "I didn't, but Jesus just told me". That word of knowledge was like putting a key in a locked-tight heart and opening it. She welcomed help after that and I spent the next year ministering to the lady, eventually taking her and her young daughter into our home to live with us.

She said she had gotten involved with a group of lesbians, who were part of a Witch Coven. Eventually, she married one of the ladies in the cult, was artificially inseminated, and gave birth to a daughter. This was a very abusive relationship and, at the time the lady called me, she had just gotten out of the hospital from being beaten badly by her partner. She was packing her belongings to leave their apartment, when a book fell off the shelf and my business card from many years before, fell out. She dialed the number, hoping it was still in service, and was surprised when I answered.

The Coven did not want to let her go and began to harass her. They came to her apartment and beat her. They ran her off the road and wrecked her car. They showed up at her place of work and slipped past security, just to intimidate her. That was when we took her into our home to protect her. One night a group of us were praying for her. As we prayed, I saw in my spirit a tall skinny man with a swastika and a pentagram on him. I also heard his first name. I told the lady what God had shown me and she said that the person I described was the Warlock of the Coven. She said his first name was what I discerned, he was tall and skinny, with a swastika tattooed on one shoulder and a pentagram on the other. I felt God had revealed this man to me, so I could target him with my prayers. I began to pray the prayers that David prayed against the enemies of God, which are recorded in the Psalms. The Warlock sent word to "cut out the mean prayers". Evidently, the devil revealed to this man what I was praying. Afterwards, I began to pray, as David prayed, that this man would get caught in his own trap. That's pretty much what happened.

In a last ditch effort to regain control of the lady, the cult kidnapped her, gang-raped her, and spoke incantations over her to be filled with demons. She had enough evidence to prosecute the Coven, but the Lord told her to forgive them. She went to the Warlock's house and told him she was not going to prosecute them, because she was forgiving them. He responded by saying, since she had let them off the hook, he would call off his people. One of the cult members refused to obey the Warlock's order and continued to harass the lady. Since this kind of insubordination could not be tolerated in the Coven, the Warlock killed the man. There was enough evidence at the crime scene for the prosecutor to issue a warrant and the police went to the Warlock's house to arrest him. When the police arrived, they found several of the Coven members in the kitchen dividing drugs to sell on the streets. The Warlock went to prison for murder and several members of the Coven went to prison for trafficking drugs. They were indeed caught in their own trap!

The last time the Coven tried to harass the lady, they parked across the street from her apartment, but would not cross the street. She finally yelled at them and asked why they were not coming over to beat her up. One of them shouted back, "You know! The angels"! She was later told that the members of the Coven saw fiery angels sitting on top of the apartment building and were afraid to approach.

I was blessed to officiate her wedding when she married a former worship leader from our church. Today, they have three children of their own, plus the daughter that she had when she lived with us.

THE SWEETEST WITCH I EVER MET

One Sunday a young lady came to our worship service dressed in black, complete with black lipstick and black fingernail polish. I met her at the door and asked if she was Goth. She said, "No, I am a witch". At the conclusion of the service, she came forward for prayer and told me her story. During the previous week, she was sitting on the bank of Sugar Creek in Johnson County Park worshipping Satan, when God revealed Himself to her. She said, up until then, she only believed in the Satan, but now believed in God. She said she had come to our church to learn more about God. Then she said, "Now I believe in Jesus too". When I asked her why she believed in Jesus, she said Jesus revealed Himself to her that day as we worshipped. Wow! Here's a person that many Christians would write-off as hopeless, but God had not written her off and actually revealed Himself to her while she was worshipping Satan. That is extreme grace! She was a very sweet person and I wondered how one so young and sweet could have gotten so involved in witchcraft. As a lady in our church and I ministered to her over the next few months, we learned she had been sexually abused by relatives during her childhood and had turned to Satan to gain power over her abusers.

One evening we went to her apartment and found her in a foul mood. She sat in the middle of the floor and would not face us. She finally said, "You know he's here, don't you"? She was referring to a demon. I replied, "Have him manifest and watch us kick his butt in Jesus name"! We suspected that she was holding onto articles from witchcraft, which prevented her from getting free. After questioning her, she produced a book of incantations, a Ouija board, and a black witch's costume, which we burned. I expected to see a major demonic manifestation as we ministered to her, but it never happened. One day, as I was praying with her, the Lord whispered in my spirit and said that her deliverance would be very gentle, and it was. I didn't want to experience a power encounter with a demon anyway and I didn't think her fragile spirit needed that.

I was blessed to pray with her to receive Jesus as her Savior and baptize her in Sugar Creek at the spot where she first experienced God. She loved children and became one of the nursery workers in our church.

No Cowboys but Plenty of Indians

The Youth Pastor organized a trip to Arizona to conduct a week of camp for teens from the Navajo and Apache Reservations, which was held at a Christian school. Jenny Sue, our daughter Sharianne, and I were part of that trip. The Youth Pastor drove a bus to the reservations and filled it with Indian teens. We did not know that Navajo and Apache people do not get along and, in fact, referred to one another as enemies. We had to keep the tribes separated or fights occurred. There were a couple of mixed race teens that neither tribe liked. We didn't know much about Indian culture, but these teens were nothing like we expected. We saw little Indian culture in them and they talked like LA Gangbangers, because they spent a lot of time watching MTV. They also had little respect for this group of white folks and refused to follow our directions.

The classes we attempted to teach were a train wreck and so were our worship services. We could barely get the Indian teens attention. They talked and laughed throughout our worship services. For three days we had very little success with anything we did. Then Wednesday came and God came to visit our week of camp. Greg and I were asked to minister to an Indian teen at the infirmary, who was exhibiting what I believe was a demonic episode. He was lying on a bunk, thrashing, and talking out of his head. Greg and I stood on opposite sides of the bunk, laid our hands on him, and prayed for release from whatever was harassing him. He soon settled down and actually went to sleep.

The evening worship followed our time of praying for the teen. I had been leading worship with my guitar and doing the preaching, but I had lost my voice. That evening, I played guitar and our teens led the singing. Since I was unable to preach, our teens gave testimonies about their relationship with Jesus. The worship service was held in a big tent and, as the first teen walked to the front to speak, the spiritual atmosphere in the tent changed. I walked to the back of the tent, because I felt like something special was about to happen and I wanted to watch the reaction of the Indian teens. As each of our teens walked to the front of the tent to give their testimony, you could see God visibly anoint them. They stood before the Indian teens and wept as they talked about their love for Jesus.

For the first time all week, the Indian teens grew quiet. As our teens continued their testimonies, some of the Indian teens began quietly weeping, which grew to loud sobbing. The Holy Spirit had descended on the week of camp. Jenny Sue and I walked over to an Indian teen named Natasha, who was the youngest teen at the week of camp and the first to start weeping. We knelt next to her chair and I asked, "Natasha, do you know what this is"? She said, "No, I have never felt like this before". I replied, "It's Jesus and He loves you". She responded, "Then I love Him". Jenny Sue and I prayed with Natasha to receive Jesus as her Savior. Then we walked to the next teen who was weeping. By then, others in our group were doing the same. That night, we prayed with a dozen Indian teens to receive Jesus as their Savior. At the end of the week, we baptized them in a stock tank. What a joy that was! In the seventeen years the school had been hosting that week of camp, they had never seen an Indian teen saved. Our group from Christ Fellowship got to witness something historic and unforgettable. The Holy Spirit had accomplished what we could not. The rest of the week of camp was altogether different.

A Farm Town and a
Plowed Field

As I shared earlier, I told the staff at Christ Fellowship I felt I would be there three years and leave to plant a church. In 1996, Jenny Sue was praying for me before we went to sleep. As she prayed, the Lord manifested powerfully and I began to weep and tremble. I remember Jenny Sue saying, "He is really touching you". Then I saw a picture in my spirit that was so powerful that it frightened me. I opened my eyes and could still see it. I saw an old farming town with grain elevators in it. As I stood in the street of this town, an English Cathedral appeared. Then, the picture changed to a field that was plowed and ready to plant. Suddenly, the picture was gone! I don't know what you would call that, but it sure sounds like a vision to me. It was like a dream while I was awake. I have had very few experiences like that in my lifetime and none as powerful as that one. I knew that God was communicating something about my ministry, so I recorded the vision in my prayer journal and prayed for understanding.

One day, I was driving from my home in Brown County to my office at Christ Fellowship in Whiteland. As I stopped at the traffic light at the intersection of 135 and 252 in Trafalgar, I looked to my right into old downtown Trafalgar where I saw the grain elevators I had seen in the vision. Then, I turned to my left and noticed that the strip mall on the corner was named Trafalgar Square, which is in England. I knew immediately that God wanted to start a church in that old farming community. I was still puzzled about the plowed field that I had seen in the vision, but one day I read in First Corinthians 3:9: "You are God's field, God's building". I knew the plowed field I had seen in the vision represented a group of people and, because the field was plowed, they were ready to plant something. I wrote in my prayer journal that day: "When I find this group of people, I will have found the core group, who will help me plant a church in Trafalgar". I shared my vision with the staff of Christ Fellowship and with a group of intercessors in the church and asked them to pray and tell me what they thought the Lord was saying.

Shortly thereafter, one of the intercessors said that she knew where my plowed field was. She said a small group met in a home near Trafalgar and offered to introduce me to the group, for I had not met any of them. When I was introduced, they asked what brought me there. I told them what God had shown me and ended by saying, "I think you are a plowed field I am looking for". By the time I was finished, the group was laughing hysterically. At the time, I wore my hair in a pony tail down to the middle of my back and was wearing a Harley sweatshirt. I wondered if the people thought I was just a dumb biker and would say, "Don't let the door hit you on your way out"! I turned to a lady named Wilma and asked, "Why is everyone laughing"? She responded, "We have all seen the same vision". That small group had been praying about planting a church in Trafalgar and waiting for God to send a Pastor, who would help them plant the church. That's how the core group came together to plant the church in Trafalgar. Jenny Sue and I began to meet regularly with the small group, as we prayed and waited for God to reveal His timing to plant the church.

A WORD FROM GOD AT A
HOSPITAL INFORMORATION DESK

A man from Christ Fellowship had been hospitalized, so I planned to go pray for him. Trish, the Administrative Assistant at Christ Fellowship, asked if she could accompany me. We drove from the church office in Whiteland to Methodist Hospital in Indianapolis. As we walked up to the information desk at the hospital, a pleasant looking black man, looked up and said, "I have a word from God for you". I didn't expect to get a word from God at a hospital information desk, but I said, "Speak it brother"! He said, "Isaiah chapter sixty-one, verses one to three, especially verse three". Then he quoted verse three: "They shall be called Oaks of Righteousness, a planting of the Lord for the display of His Splendor". I thanked him for his words, which were confirmation of something that I had been experiencing in prayer. I had been seeing a huge Oak Tree in my spirit when I prayed. I had drawn a picture of it in my prayer journal, but I did not know what it meant until that day.

Neither Trish nor I had brought a Bible, so I suggested we stop at the Hospital Chapel, where we could find a Bible to check out Isaiah 61:1-3. There, on a table at the front of the chapel, a Bible was laying open. It was opened to Isaiah chapter sixty-one! I trembled and wept! God had revealed another piece of the puzzle He had been sharing about planting a church. He is so faithful!

CONFIRMATION FROM A COUNSELOR

I was invited by a group from Christ Fellowship to hear a Counselor speak at a rally in Indianapolis. I had not met this man, whose name was Terry. After a time of worship, Terry walked back to where I was seated, pointed to me, and said, "You're a Pastor". Then he corrected himself, "No, you're an Assistant Pastor and God wants you to know there is a flock with your name on it". The group who came with me began to snicker, because they knew I was praying about planting a church. The words Terry spoke were more confirmation that God was indeed calling me to plant a church.

A Powerful Dream

One night, I dreamed I rode a horse somewhere to preach, but I could not leave, because I could not find the horse. As I write, I can still see that dream in my mind from 1996. I recorded the dream in my prayer journal and began to pray for understanding. I shared the dream with a very discerning Pastor who, without hesitation, began to interpret the dream. He said vehicles that carry us, like the horse, represent the Holy Spirit's leading. He said I couldn't find the horse, because it was not time to leave the place where I was ministering. He then applied the dream to my situation and said, it was the Holy Spirit who led me to Christ Fellowship and the Holy Spirit would lead me out. He also said, the Holy Spirit respects spiritual authority in the church and the Holy Spirit would tell the Senior Pastor when it was time to release me to plant a church. That's exactly what happened! Though the Senior Pastor was reluctant to see me leave Christ Fellowship, one day he informed me that his wife said it was time to release me to plant the church in Trafalgar. He also said he had talked with the elders and they had agreed to pay my full salary for six months and then half my salary for another six months to help get the church started. What a blessing that was!

A DOWNLOAD OF REVELATION

I took a week off from Christ Fellowship to seek the Lord and do some planning for the new church. On Monday morning, I sat on the floor with my back against the couch listening to a worship CD, with my hands raised in worship. In a flood of revelation, the Lord said the church would be called New Covenant Fellowship, the mission statement would come from Isaiah 61:1-3, and the logo of the church would be an Oak Tree.

UNDER THE OAK TREE

New Covenant met for the first time in September of 1997 at the home of Bruce and Frieda Dowler, who lived near Trafalgar. The small group I mentioned earlier, met at this home. We met under the shade of an Oak tree, which was very fitting, since the logo of New Covenant was an Oak tree. Sixty-one people were in attendance. As I write this section of the book, I just caught the significance of the number of people who attended our first worship service. New Covenant's mission statement came from Isaiah chapter SIXTY-ONE and SIXTY-ONE people attended our first worship service! It took me twenty-six years to notice that! Wow, even a blind bird could follow that trail of crumbs!

It was exciting to feel like we were finally a church. Bruce and Frieda had a nice swimming pool, which soon became a baptistry, where we baptized several folk the first month of New Covenant's history. We worshipped under the Oak tree through the month of September and most of October, but knew that we soon needed to find an indoor meeting place, because the worship leader wore gloves to play his keyboard at our last outdoor service.

We soon rented a building in Trafalgar for our Sunday morning worship service, known as "Miss Betty's", a dinner theater and county line dance venue. We met there for several months, before moving to the "yellow house" next to The Place For Hair, a hair salon located on

SR 135 in Trafalgar. When giving directions to New Covenant, we told people to look for the yellow house next to The Place For Hair.

Although the yellow house was not ideal place for a church, we made it work. We worshipped in three adjoining rooms, which made it hard to see the people seated in adjacent rooms, but I found a spot to preach, where I could be seen by most. Coffee was usually brewing in the kitchen, which added a nice fragrance to our worship service. We had some great times worshipping in the yellow house and squeezed up to a hundred people into the house.

LOBO

While meeting in the yellow house, Rick, whose biker name was Lobo, became part of New Covenant. At a small group meeting, our daughter told us her friend Rick had terminal cancer and was on hospice care, given six months to live. She invited him to the meeting, but he declined, saying he was too emotional. She then asked if we could pray for him at the meeting and he consented. After we prayed fervently for Lobo, he called Sharianne to ask if we had just been praying for him. When she said yes, he told her that an awesome peace had come over him and he was no longer afraid to die. Sharianne asked if she could come to his home and pray for him and he consented.

When Sharianne prayed for Lobo, she said the Lord did not lead her to pray for his physical healing, but for his emotional healing. Lobo told me that when she began praying, her hand felt like it was burning his chest and he was about to ask her to remove it. He opened his eyes and found that she was not touching him. After that, Lobo began to get better. A year later, his oncologist could not find a cancer cell in his body. He once showed me his cancer screen and it looked like a target of a man who had been shot with a shotgun. He had cancer all over his body, but now it was gone!

Lobo became an integral part of New Covenant and one of my best friends ever. We soon ordained him Assistant Pastor. We had earlier ordained Bruce as Assistant Pastor. Bruce, Lobo, and I ministered very well together. We also ordained Mary, to oversee ministry to the ladies of our church.

Lobo was a perfect blend of book smart and street wise, having been involved in almost every kind of dysfunctional behavior imaginable. This made him well-qualified to minister to the dysfunctional people that New Covenant was attracting. We referred to New Covenant as a Spiritual ER. And, it was! We asked God to send people other churches did not want and promised to love them and minister to them. And, He did! Lobo had been clean and sober for several years and helped many people find sobriety through Alcoholics Anonymous. He had also ridden with Fifth Chapter, a clean and sober biker group, named after the fifth chapter of the big book of Alcoholics Anonymous.

Our Garage Church

The time came to move from the yellow house, for we had definitely outgrown it. Bruce found a building for rent in downtown Trafalgar that he thought would make a good home for our church. The building, a car repair shop for many years, was very dirty and needed a lot of work. We rented the building and joyfully began remodeling it to become Our Garage Church. The building had a large open room, two smaller rooms, a kitchen, and a restroom. After we covered a grease pit and built a stage over a car lift in the large room, it became our worship area. We also added another bathroom, remodeled the kitchen, carpeted most of the building, and did extensive painting and decorating. When we were finished, the old garage actually looked like a place of worship.

When the building was a car repair shop, it was heated with a coal stove, so the attic above the suspended ceiling was filled with soot. One day, after pulling electrical wiring through the attic, I climbed down looking like a black man. I was in the attic one day wiring a junction box for electrical receptacles in the wall below, where Bruce was installing the receptacles. I had tripped a breaker in the electrical panel and thought the circuit was dead. However, I had tripped the wrong breaker and the circuit was live. As I connected two wires in the junction box, a spark jumped across my fingers. I was not grounded, sitting on a rafter in the attic, so I was not shocked. However, Bruce was well-grounded working on his knees on the concrete floor below. As the spark jumped between my fingers, I heard Bruce say, "Ouch"! That's when I discovered I had tripped the wrong breaker. Oops!

Remodeling the old garage was great fellowship with the many volunteers who took part. As our garage church took shape, our excitement about the next chapter of New Covenant Fellowship's history grew.

My Spiritual Journey

Lobo began attracting people in recovery to our church and suggested we start a recovery group. That seemed like an excellent idea and I encouraged him to go for it. His cousin Nancy, also part of our church, teamed with him to launch the group. The group was called "My Spiritual Journey" because, as Lobo insisted, the road to recovery is a spiritual journey. The group met at another building New Covenant rented, which we called "The Gathering Place". The first meeting was well attended and Lobo explained the group's purpose and outlined the ground rules. He stated that the group's Higher Power had a name, Jesus! He went on to say that if anyone was offended by that, they were in the wrong group. Much like the volleyball league at Franklin Memorial, My Spiritual Journey proved to be a great "side door" entry point to our church. Soon, we were seeing people saved and baptized because of the recovery group.

One Sunday after worship, we baptized several people who came to know Christ through our recovery group. I got permission from a local Pastor to use their baptistry. However, he had failed to tell the Youth Pastor. Several of our people rode motorcycles to the church for the baptisms. When the Youth Pastor, who was alone at the church, saw these bikers roll into the parking lot, he locked the doors and called the Senior Pastor. After talking with the Senior Pastor, the Youth Pastor apologetically opened the doors.

Lobo and I stood on either side of the people and baptized them together. We baptized a lady named Becky, who had come a long way in her spiritual journey to recovery. Lobo told me later that he sensed something dark and evil come out of her when we raised her from the water. Lobo was very perceptive spiritually, so when Lobo said something, I believed it. The next Sunday, Becky gave her testimony at our worship service. She began by saying, "Hi, I'm Becky and I am an alcoholic". The congregation responded, "Hi Becky". Then we all laughed because we realized that our congregation had taken on the style of an AA Meeting, which suited us just fine. Dang, I miss those days!

Want to sit by a Bank Robber or a Former Lesbian?

I was asked to invite a lady to worship, who had just begun working at a Dry Cleaning business next to The Place For Hair. Her name was Rosie and I had met her years earlier when I conducted a revival meeting at a church in Morgantown. Rosie was glad to see me, but said she was not in a good place with God and felt "too bad to come to our church". In one of those Holy Spirit inspired moments of brilliance, I asked, "Would you like to sit by a former bank robber or a former lesbian"? She looked startled and blurted out, "You're kidding"? I responded, "No I am not kidding"! Rosie felt she could fit in at a church like that and came to worship with us the next Sunday. She became a very faithful part of New Covenant, a close friend to all, and a real prayer warrior. And, she became close friends with the former bank robber and often sat next to him.

BAND OF BROTHERS

One of the coolest things we did at New Covenant was our Band of Brothers meetings, referred to as BOB meetings. BOB grew from the video series "Wild At Heart", by John Eldredge. This excellent series covers the identity and purpose of a man from God's perspective. At each meeting, we viewed a portion of the series and then opened the meeting for discussion. The discussion was raw and honest. Occasionally, we saw some incredible displays of emotion as men shared their wounds and received prayer. I still vividly remember two of the burliest men in our group, hugging, crying, and praying for each other. I think some serious "father wounds" were healed that night, for both of them had been abandoned by their father when they were young. When the series ended, it was obvious that we had developed a fellowship that needed to continue, which led to the creation of our BOB meetings.

Though the meetings were somewhat non-religious, the BOB meetings were intensely spiritual. We sat around a campfire, smoked cigars, and talked about Jesus. Our agenda was to have little agenda, just let the Holy Spirit orchestrate. After a short worship time with guitar, I simply asked, "How are you guys doing tonight"? What usually followed was gut-honest sharing and ministry. As men shared their struggles, the band of brothers offered words of encouragement and prayed for them. This group of men did indeed become a Band of Brothers, with a unique and special bond. Our wives didn't understand the cigar smoking, so we explained that it was a "man's thing"! Our BOB meetings were indeed a man's thing and we grew in our understanding of our role as Godly men.

The J.C. Riders

While I was still at Franklin Memorial, I wanted to get involved in ministering to bikers, but I didn't think I could do that riding my Honda Rebel. A lot of hard-core bikers hated Honda Rebels. I needed something with a little more credibility in the biker world—a Harley Davidson Sportster, but I did not have the five-hundred dollar deposit needed to order the bike. On my way to Pennsylvania to preach a revival meeting, I prayed about my desire to become involved in biker ministry and asked the Lord if He would please provide the five-hundred dollar deposit for a new bike.

The revival meeting went very well. Each night the church took an offering designated as compensation for my preaching. At the closing service, the Pastor invited me to the stage, where he thanked me for my preaching and gave me a check for my labor. Then, he handed me a second check, which he said was a gift from the church to use as I pleased. I unfolded the check to find it was written for exactly five-hundred dollars. I thanked the church profusely and shared my plan for biker ministry. I praised God all the way back to Indiana and could hardly wait to get to Big Red Harley Davidson in Bloomington to order my new Harley Sportster. Hallelujah, God is good!

When my new Harley arrived, I joined the Highway Crusaders Motorcycle Ministry in Bloomington. I rode with the Crusaders for a couple of years, ministering at many biker events. Bikers don't always play well with one another and that was the case with the Highway Crusaders. Personality conflicts caused the group to collapse. I then began riding with the Unchained Gang Motorcycle Ministry, but I never patched with them. "Patched", means to complete the probate period and be awarded a group's patch. My desire was to start a Motorcycle Ministry called the J.C. Riders, which had been my dream since I first rode with the Highway Crusaders. I was just waiting for God's timing to start the group.

After we started New Covenant Fellowship, I felt like I was in the right place to start the J.C. Riders, but I was waiting for God to send the right people to lead the group. One Sunday, Jenny Sue and I invited Lobo over for lunch and, after we had eaten, I asked Lobo if he would like to ride Jenny Sue's Kawasaki Eliminator. He was more than excited, because he did not own a bike at the time. Jenny Sue rode with me on my Harley and Lobo followed on Jenny Sue's Kawasaki. In my mirrors, I could see Lobo had a huge smile on his face. Soon, he began looking for a bike, but could not borrow the money to purchase it. Since the Lord had blessed me with the deposit for my bike, I felt like I needed to pay that forward, so I co-signed for Lobo's new Harley. I also helped his cousin Nancy to buy a bike. I soon shared with Lobo my dream for the J.C. Riders and asked if he would like to be part of the group and help get it started. He was more than willing, as was his cousin Nancy. The two of them were invaluable in getting the J.C. Riders started. I had drawn a design for a patch for the group, which depicted an Eagle with three crosses gripped in its talons and a rocker that said J.C. Riders. Lobo and Nancy digitized the patch and found a company to embroider them. We sewed our J.C. Rider patch onto the lower left corner of a Christian Flag patch. This idea came from Barry Mason, who before his conversion to Christ,

SURPRISED BY THE CALL OF GOD

was the President of the Atlanta chapter of the Hell's Angels. He encouraged this as a sign of unity among motorcycle ministries. I got to spend some time with Barry at the Boogie one year and was really impressed with the brother. Boy, did he have stories to tell!

Soon, Greg joined our group and was appointed Road Captain. He had eyes like a hawk and always remembered directions. We dubbed him "Slomo", after we watched him drop his bike in slow motion on the Blue Ridge Parkway. Our group pulled into a rest stop on the Parkway and there was sand on the asphalt. When Greg put his foot down, it slowly slid in the sand until he dropped his bike. We were laughing so hard that it took several seconds to rush over and get Greg's bike off him. So, Greg became Slomo, the biker who crashed in slow motion. Lobo and I rode to Indianapolis to help with a street ministry and a lady from the neighborhood told me I was purty, so I was dubbed "Purty". Jenny Sue became "Scoop", since she managed Miller's Ice Cream House and scooped ice cream. Nancy became "Lucy".

BRAD AND DEB

A lady named Deb, began worshiping with New Covenant and soon brought her boyfriend Brad. I immediately liked Brad, who had served in Vietnam in the Marine Corp, where he received a leg injury when the jeep he was driving ran over an IED. The General, who was riding with him, was killed. He loved music, had a killer voice, and played several stringed instruments. As Brad and Deb continued to worship with us, I would occasionally see Brad wipe tears when a worship song touched him. Before long, I invited Brad to play bass guitar in our praise band and Deb to sing. Brad and Deb also began riding with the JC Riders, but had not yet patched. The group went for a ride almost every Sunday after church and usually ended up at the Ice Cream House in Nashville, or at our house in Brown County. After one of our Sunday rides, as Brad sat next to me at our kitchen table, I asked him if there was anything keeping him from becoming a Christian. In his deep gruff voice, he answered, "Nope"! I asked if he would like to accept Christ as his Savior right then and he said, "Yep"! As I prayed with him to receive Jesus as his Savior, his tears flowed. It was a happy day when I was privileged to baptize Brad. After that, he cried a lot. One day he came to praise band practice and said, "I don't know what's wrong with me, I cry all the time". We prayed for him and he cried. I think Jesus was helping Brad process a lot of emotional stuff.

Brad and Deb both patched with the J.C. Riders and became part of our ministry. Brad was dubbed "Sweet Pea", after Deb told us a story about him accosting a man in Kroger for verbally abusing his wife. Deb said the wife was trying to shop, with a child in one arm and another in the shopping cart, while her husband followed behind swearing at her. Brad got in the guy's face and said, "Pick up one of those kids and start helping your wife, or I'm gonna grab a can of peas and beat you unconscious"! The man picked up one of the kids and started helping his wife. You do not want to abuse a woman in Brad's presence. Good for him!

TIN MAN

The first time Tin Man came to our church, he entered with a group of bikers and I did not notice him until I walked up to the stage to preach. Looking out over the crowd, I saw a biker, about one size smaller than a Grizzly Bear. He had a shaved head and a long goatee, braided in pig tails. He was sitting right in front of me, staring intently, with his face frozen in a frown. As I began my sermon, his expression did not change, which I found a bit intimidating! As I continued to preach, he began to nod agreement. By the time I finished my sermon, he was fist-pumping agreement and saying amen. Little did I know, when I first met Tin Man, he would become one of my best friends ever—someone who always "had my six". His name was James, but he was called Tin Man, not because he had no heart, but because he was a HIVAC tech and fabricated a lot of sheet metal. Tin Man had a big heart and loved everyone. He soon patched with the J.C. Riders and became very faithful to our biker ministry. Tin Man and I attended a couple of biker events together every year. I always felt very safe with him. At one such event, I heard Tin Man ask a biker, "Have you ever accepted Jesus as your personal Savior"? Tin Man was a bold witness for Jesus!

So many bikers worshipped with New Covenant in those days, that the locals dubbed us "The Biker Church". Sometimes people would ask if I preached at that biker church and I would respond, "No, most of our people drive cars".

POPCORN AND JODY

O n Saturdays afternoons, I often rode my bike into Nashville and sat on the wall in front of the Court House to talk with bikers. Back in the day, the street in front of the Court House was lined with bikes and the wall was lined with bikers. I met a couple of bikers one day, whose biker names were Popcorn and Jody. Popcorn was a rough guy who had operated bars on the west side of Indianapolis, where outlaw bikers hung out. He once said, "I don't want to say that my bars were rough, but we passed-out guns when people came in". Soon after I met Popcorn and Jody, I knew that I should probably not try to witness to Popcorn, or he would throw me under a bus. Once, a man tried to give Popcorn a Christian tract and Popcorn gave the man the cussing of his life.

I had a dream about Popcorn and Jody shortly after I met them. I dreamed I was sitting with them on the wall, when Jody pointed at a bike on the curb and remarked that it was a really nice Narrow Glide, a Harley with Sportster front end and a Big Twin rear end. The weekend after I had that dream, I was sitting with Popcorn and Jody on the wall and Jody DID point to a bike on the curb and say, "That's a really nice Narrow Glide". I got goose bumps, because I knew that meeting Popcorn and Jody was no coincidence. Popcorn eventually told me that he was on disability for congestive heart failure. In fact, he had been given a year to live several years before I met him. After that, I always asked him how he felt and told him that I was praying for him. He didn't seem to know how to react to that. In the course of time, Popcorn and Jody met other members of the J.C. Riders. I didn't try to preach to Popcorn and Jody, I just loved them.

One Saturday afternoon, while sitting with Popcorn and Jody on the wall, he said, "I'm gonna smoke one more cigarette and if no bikes come by, I'm gonna go home". Then he turned to me and asked, "What time did you say that church starts"? The next day, Popcorn and Jody rolled up to New Covenant on their bike. Jody came in for worship, but Popcorn sat on his bike across the street. When the service was over, I went out to ask him why he had not come in for the service. He told me he forgot that he was carrying his pistol. I responded, "Popcorn, half the people in there are carrying". The next Sunday, Popcorn and Jody were both in worship at New Covenant and really seemed to enjoy it. Jody had some bad history with churches and Popcorn had only been in church a few times for weddings. At one of those weddings, Popcorn and the best man mooned the congregation. Popcorn and Jody had only worshipped with New Covenant a few Sundays, when Popcorn came forward during ministry time to surrender his life to Jesus. I had the honor of praying with him to receive Jesus as his Savior and baptizing him. When Jody watched me immerse Popcorn, she said, "That's not what they did when they baptized me, I want that". So I baptized Jody also.

THE BOOGIE

Riding with the J.C. Riders is one of the most enjoyable things I have done in my entire life! One of my favorite events was The Boogie, where we ministered with several other biker ministries. This event attracted up to 40,000 bikers and provided lots of opportunities to minister. One year, the J.C. Riders and a couple of other biker ministries prayed over the Boogie grounds before the event started. That was special! This event, originally held in Beanblossom, later moved to Lawrence County. Christian biker groups usually hung out at the Christian Riders booth, where we passed out water, coffee, and the love of Jesus. One year, my friend Sparky, who was at that time riding with the Unchained Gang, asked me to pray with a young man who wanted to accept Christ as his Savior. As people walked by naked and stoned, I laid my hand on the young man and began to pray. He trembled and wept and his voice broke when he repeated a confession of faith. I remember thinking how amazing it was for the Holy Spirit to manifest so powerfully in such a dark place. But, why not?! The light always shines the brightest against a background of darkness.

People asked me how I could go to those evil biker events. It was because God anointed to be there and I never felt more spiritually dangerous! Seeing the Christian patches and pins on our vests, bikers would often apologize for their behavior. Once, a biker walked up to Lobo and I and began weeping as he asked us to pray for him.

Another time, a group of us were following our friend Midget, as he dragged his huge cross through the Boogie grounds. A biker watched curiously and then said, "You guys have bigger balls than anyone I ever met. I would give anything to be like that"! Midget laid down his cross and walked over to talk with the man, who immediately began to weep. Often, within minutes of meeting someone, we were praying with them. We regularly wore a tee shirt that read "Jesus died for bikers too". I know that is true, because Jesus made His presence known at so many biker events. I only live two miles from where the Boogie was held in Beanblossom, but I camped with my biker brothers and sisters, just to be around them. They were some of the boldest, most authentic Christians I have ever met. Before their conversion to Christ, many of them rode with outlaw gangs and have incredible testimonies.

RUN TO THE SMOKYS

One of the highlights of our summer was the J.C. Riders "Run to the Smokys", which was a weeklong camping and riding event, with up to a dozen riders taking part. I loved riding in formation! Slomo, our Road Captain, was usually in the lead and I often rode Drag in the rear. The Road Captain and the Drag watched for dangers that could come from the front or rear. Other riders were staggered in a tight, but safe formation. Our destination was usually a campground on the banks of the Little River near the Smoky Mountains National Park. As we rolled into the campground one year, we really upset a family from Ohio who were camping next to us. I'll tell you more about that later.

We had a destination each day on the twisty roads of the Smokys. We loved to ride the Cherahola Skyway, the Smoky Mountains Parkway, the National Park, but our favorite ride was "The Tail of the Dragon", a section of US129 that has 318 curves in 11 miles. At one hairpin curve, Jenny Sue was on her Harley on the downside of the curve and I was on my Harley at the top. I could hear Jenny Sue screaming down below as she rode through that tight curve. That was the first time she rode her Harley through the dragon and, when we got back to camp, she disappeared in our tent and slept for four hours. Jenny Sue wants it noted: She did not drop her bike on the Dragon! Good girl!

Deal's Gap, a biker hangout at the Tail of the Dragon, is a special place. A tree at Deal's Gap is designated the "Tree of Shame" and has hundreds of bike parts hanging on it from crashes on the Dragon. Slomo almost hit a Black Bear on the Dragon and I don't think that would have turned out well. We loved hanging out at Deal's Gap, swapping tales with the bikers who gas-up, camp, eat at the restaurant, browse the bike shop, or stay at the motel. Brad and I rode to Deal's Gap one summer and stayed at the motel. One morning, we got up early to ride the Cherahola Skyway, which wanders across the tops of the mountains from Robbinsville, NC to Telico Planes, TN at an elevation of about five-thousand feet. As we rode through the lower elevations of the Skyway, we were literally riding through clouds. I stopped to ask Brad what he thought about that. He was so overwhelmed he was crying.

Our J.C. Rider trips to the Smokys always included a "cager", who pulled a trailer. A car or a truck is called a cage, because when compared to a bike, it's like riding in a cage. The cager carried a lot of our gear, which included the guitars we played around the campfire in the evenings. The trailer was needed in case someone's bike broke down. In the evenings, we sat around the campfire, played guitars, worshipped, shared, and prayed. One night, this group of tough-looking bikers poured their hearts out and, as Brad says, "Boohooed like babies". I gave a J.C. Riders brochure, which included my address, to the family from Ohio who camped next to us. A few weeks later, I got a letter from the family. They said they were really upset when we pulled in next to them at the campground and started to leave, but felt humbled and stayed, when we hung up a Christian flag. They admitted to eavesdropping on our conversations, which they said really inspired them. The letter ended by thanking us for the Christian lessons this group of tough-looking bikers had taught them that week.

A Grand Entrance at a Men's Conference

During my J.C. Rider days, I was invited to speak at a men's conference at a church in Whiteland. They explicitly asked me to dress in biker clothes and ride my Harley down the center aisle of the church before I spoke. I gladly accepted, since I did not have much experience with riding my Harley in church. Ha! When it was time for me to speak, they opened the front doors of the building and I roared in on my Harley, down the center aisle to the front of the sanctuary. At that time, I had slash cut drag pipes on my bike, which are about the loudest exhaust pipes on the market. I stopped at the front of the sanctuary, revved the motor, and racked the pipes several times. The sound reverberated through the building like cannon blasts and a flame shot out of the pipes, as the sanctuary filled with the smell of Harley exhaust. I didn't do a burn-out, which would probably have been inappropriate on their nice carpet. I don't remember the topic of my sermon that day, but I sure remember my grand entrance. Man that was fun!

LOSING LOBO

Earlier in the book, I wrote about my daughter praying for Lobo and his cancer disappearing. Lobo lived cancer-free for about ten years, before the cancer returned. I often prayed that God would give Lobo fifteen bonus years, like He did Hezekiah. Lobo got ten bonus years and they were good. During those years, Lobo, the J.C. Riders, and I rode our bikes all over the country ministering to people. Once, when the J.C. Riders were riding in Tennessee, we pulled into a motel where Lobo spotted a man with radiation markings on his neck from cancer treatments. Lobo was encouraging that man and praying for him by the time I got off my bike. It was almost as if Lobo could smell cancer and he ministered to many people who suffered with it.

One of my most memorable rides with Lobo was to a Pastor's Conference in Charlotte, North Carolina. It was cold on the way to Charlotte, but the ride home was spectacular! On our way home, we decided to ride every twisty road we could find through the mountains of North Carolina and get totally lost. We did manage to get lost and, when we stopped to get our bearings, I looked up at the road sign which read "Whetstine Road". Wow! When I got home, I researched the area online and found I have distant relatives there. We stopped at a small mom and pop motel somewhere in the mountains and stayed the night. A shiny steel-covered diner next door to the motel had great food. I would love to go back, but I have no idea where we were. During my morning shower, I found a huge Wolf Spider in the bathroom. Lobo hated spiders and I knew that if he saw it, he would skip his shower. I whacked the spider with a towel and hundreds of baby spiders, riding on its back, scattered across the floor. I scooped up as many spiders as I could and did not mention it to Lobo until we left. We planned to get on the Blue Ridge Parkway near Ashville, but a rockslide had closed the Parkway, so we detoured through the Pisgah National Forest and I am glad we did, because it was a gorgeous ride up to the highest point of the Blue Ridge Parkway. We rode the Parkway to its end at Cherokee, NC and snaked our way around the south end of the Smokys to Deal's Gap, where we ran into rain on the Tail of the Dragon. The rain continued through Tennessee into Kentucky and we finally found motel with a vacancy in Kentucky. I fell to my knees at the check-in desk and said, "Thank you Jesus"! In spite of the rain, it was an awesome trip. I really miss those days.

The doctors started Lobo on an experimental drug given by infusion. I drove him to the hospital and prayed over every bag of medicine infused into his veins, but the treatment was unsuccessful. Lobo began making preparations to die. That was a sad time in my life. Lobo passed in 2006, after he had planned his memorial service and burial in great detail. I preached his funeral, which was attended by a large crowd of his friends and family. One of the few days in January warm enough to ride, the funeral procession included many motorcycles. Lobo's body was carried to the family cemetery at Dixon Chapel in a glass-covered hearse pulled by a Harley trike. His headstone has a picture of him on his bike in Monument Valley, with the logos of the Fifth Chapter Motorcycle Club and the J.C. Riders Motorcycle Ministry on either side of his picture. His fully-charged cell phone was placed in his pocket before he was buried, so we could call him and hear him say, "I'm kinda busy and I can't come to the phone right now". We called his cell phone and left messages until the battery died.

It still doesn't seem like Lobo can be gone, because he was so bigger than life. I think of him almost every day. I still expect him to call and say, "Hey Dude, let's go for a ride". Jenny Sue and I often quote him—we call those quotes "Loboisms". One of our favorites has to do with criticism. When someone would criticize Lobo, he would say, "When you're through measuring me, can I use that yardstick on you"?

The J.C. Riders were just not the same after Lobo passed and his cousin Nancy moved back to Missouri. But, I have great memories of a truly unique and special guy! I love you Lobo and I look forward to seeing you again in the next life.

LOSING POPCORN

Much like Lobo, Popcorn lived on borrowed time for several years after the doctors gave him a year to live. As we watched Popcorn fade and grow weaker, it became hard for him to ride his bike, which frustrated him. He had ridden a motorcycle most of his life. Popcorn had some bouts with illness but usually bounced back. Leukemia finally took him. I drove to the hospital in Indianapolis when he was admitted. When I arrived, Jody ran home to take care of something and left me to sit with Popcorn. The doctors had started him on chemotherapy that day, but his weakened heart was having difficulty bearing the stress. He was shaking badly and could not feed himself, so I fed him. I could tell that it really humbled him, but it was an honor for me. I stayed at the hospital fairly late, but needed to get back to Brown County. As I left Popcorn that night, I hugged him and told him how much I loved him. He responded with, "I love you too Don". I did not know, those would be the last words I would hear him speak to me. Soon after I got home, Jody called to tell me he had passed.

Popcorn's memorial service was a joyful celebration. I had a few brief remarks at the beginning and then his friends shared memories of him. Popcorn was a character and many humorous stories were shared. One of my favorites was shared by Super Dave, a biker who had ridden with Popcorn for many years. Super Dave said that he and Popcorn were riding in Illinois and stopped at a bar, where a kid with a rainbow colored Mohawk hairdo came in. Popcorn kept looking over at the kid until the kid became irritated. He walked over to Popcorn and asked, "Have you got a problem with me old man"? Popcorn replied, "No, it's just that I once had sex with a peacock and I thought you might be my son". That's classic Popcorn! As I said, he was a character!

I am happy that I took time to sit on the wall in front of the Court House with Popcorn and Jody and had opportunity to introduce Popcorn to Jesus. Otherwise, I don't think he would be in Heaven. I came to love him like a brother and I am encouraged that I will see him again. There must be a rowdy section in Heaven for people like Popcorn and Lobo. I am sure I will find them there. I'll just listen for a lot of people laughing and telling stories.

Moving new Covenant to Franklin

After New Covenant met in Trafalgar for several years, we began to think we should move our church to Franklin, where most of our people lived. We located a building in Franklin that we thought would meet our needs. It had been a dance studio but, after a fore-closure, belonged to a bank. We thought one large room would make a great worship area and another large room could become our fellowship hall. It had an office area, two rooms that we could use for a nursery and children's church, and a very nice kitchen. The bank had earlier listed the building for $600,000, but had no takers at that price, so they dropped the price to $300,000 to unload it. That price was well within our budget, so we bought the building. We applied for a variance to use the building as a church, which was granted, and also filed the paperwork to take the property off the tax rolls.

The New Covenant crowd was hard-working and resourceful, so we did the remodeling ourselves. We built a stage and sound booth in the worship area, added walk-in closets along one wall of the fellowship hall, installed crash bars on the exit doors to comply with the Fire Marshall, and painted all the interior walls of the building. We really enjoyed working together to transform the building into the new worship center for New Covenant Fellowship. We put up a large sign in front of the building which read:

The Filling Station

The Home of New Covenant Fellowship

At the inaugural meeting of New Covenant in the Filling Station, several of my high school classmates came to visit, which was organized by my classmate Patti Wood. What a blessing! Patti passed away a few days before I am writing this section of the book. She was a beautiful, elegant, and kind lady, a friend to all. I am sad she is gone, but I know where she is and will see her again.

New Covenant Fellowship only met in the Filling Station for a few years, but those were good years and a lot of great ministry took place there. God had a plan prepared for the next phase of my life that I could not have imagined. That's my next story.

RETIREMENT

I was the Senior Pastor of New Covenant Fellowship for seventeen years, but at age seventy, I was feeling the fatigue of fifty years of fulltime ministry. I also felt like the church had wandered from its original vision. One day, I was asking the Lord if I should cast a new vision for New Covenant and He spoke with great clarity. He said it was not for me to cast a new vision for the church, because I would not be there to implement it. I asked the Lord what that meant and He told me it was time for me to retire from fulltime ministry. I asked the Lord, "What about New Covenant"? The Lord said to merge New Covenant with another church in Franklin and then retire.

While New Covenant was meeting in Franklin, I became part of a great Pastors Fellowship, which included several Church Planters like me. At one of our meetings, I shared what God had spoken to me and asked for prayer. When I got to the part about merging New Covenant with another church in Franklin before I retired, one of the Pastors slapped his hand against his chest, gasped, and began to weep. He said, "That is such a Kingdom thing and it so resonates with my heart". At that moment, I knew New Covenant should merge with that Pastor and his church. When I called the Pastor to discuss merging our churches, he said he knew why I was calling before he picked up the phone. We prayed together and soon got the leaders of our churches together to pray and discuss a merger. Within 20 days, we had merged the two churches and I was free to retire from fulltime ministry. This church had actually considered buying the building before New Covenant did, when the bank was asking $600.000, but they could not afford that. We passed the building on to this church, after we bought it for $300.000, did extensive remodeling, and paid down the principle. Since this was a merger, there was little paper work to be done, and the church simply took over the mortgage payments. Years later, they merged with another church in Franklin. There has been a lot of church DNA in that building.

The people of New Covenant hosted a wonderful retirement party for Jenny Sue and I at the Filling Station. A huge crowd of people attended, who had been part of our lives and ministry for many years. They shared words of gratitude and encouragement and prayed blessings over us, which was very touching.

One of the last things I did at New Covenant was to perform a wedding ceremony for Tin Man and his Fiancé Mabel. The wedding was a lot of fun. We ate, laughed, and danced until late into the evening. I asked the DJ to play "Smoke Gets in Your Eyes" and Jenny Sue and I danced to one of our favorite songs from high school. I felt like I was seventeen again. As I was leaving the building that night, someone informed me that one of the thermostats in the building was not working properly. It gave me great pleasure to say, "I'm sorry, but I am retired and I don't work here anymore". Lol!

LOSING TIN MAN

A few years after I retired from New Covenant, Tin Man called to tell me he had been diagnosed with ALS and given a year to live. He and his wife were devastated by the diagnosis, as was I. I drove to Indy to pray with Tin Man and Mabel. Over the next year, he began to lose motor skills and was pretty discouraged when he could no longer ride his Harley, for he had ridden Harleys most of his life. In spite of his disease, Tin Man retained a good attitude about his situation. One day, a mutual friend and I drove to Indy to take him out for lunch at the Choc-cola Café, one of Tin Man's favorite restaurants, a cute little place with a lot of James Dean, Elvis, and Beatles memorabilia on the walls. We laughed and carried on until I thought we might be thrown out. It was a memorable day. Jenny Sue and I later ate with Tin Man and Mabel at the Café.

Tin Man had grown up in a non-instrumental Church of Christ and loved to sing the old hymns. During his last year of life, he regularly called and asked me to sing Victory in Jesus with him over the phone. It gave him great joy and comfort to sing that hymn with me. Hospitalized several times during his last year, he became increasingly incapacitated, but did not totally lose his ability to communicate, which was a blessing. Jenny Sue and I drove to the VA Hospital in Indy a couple of days before he passed. He was wearing an oxygen mask and could barely speak. We asked if we could sing Victory in

Jesus with him and he nodded approval. As we sang the hymn, I could see Tin Man's mouth moving beneath the oxygen mask, as he whispered the words of the song. I kissed him on the forehead, told him how much I loved him, asked him to say hello to Lobo and Popcorn, and said my last good bye. Tin Man passed almost a year to the day from the time of his diagnosis.

Much like Popcorn and Lobo, Tin Man's funeral was a joyous celebration of a life well lived. Jenny Sue and I sang Victory in Jesus, a fellow biker and I preached, and Tin Man's two daughters danced to the closing song. I am so grateful that Tin Man was my friend. What a blessing he was to me! I am sure that I will find him with Lobo and Popcorn in that rowdy section of Heaven. I love you Tin Man and I miss you!

BLESSED RETIREMENT

I retired from fulltime ministry in 2013. Jenny Sue and I worked our butts off to be out of debt at retirement and accomplished that goal. Shortly after I retired, we paid cash for a 2008 Ford Ranger pickup and a 2006 Suzuki ATV. It felt good to be in a place of financial freedom. We aren't rich, but we don't owe anyone. For the next year, I worked around the Beanblossom Hobby Farm and had one of the most restful years of my life. I worked on our house, gardened, tended our chickens, hunted, foraged for mushrooms, hiked the forests, hung out with friends, and cut firewood. Some days, I purposely did nothing!

Mountain Top High

Shortly after I retired, I flew to Oregon to climb mountains with Jenny Sue's brother Lee. He had been after me for years to come to Oregon and climb Mount Thielsen, his favorite mountain. Thielsen is located not far from Crater Lake and the Rogue River, two of my favorite places in Oregon. Our climb was in July, after the snow had melted on the mountains and temps were warmer at high altitudes. Lee is a retired teacher and one of his teacher buddies accompanied us. It was one-hundred degrees at the base of Thielsen, but we expected the temps to cool considerably as we made our ascent. However, temps were not much cooler at higher altitudes, which made the climb much harder and required more water than expected. The peak of Thielsen looms about ten-thousand feet above sea level and the view is spectacular. Just below the peak, we had to carefully make out way across a section of loose stone, sliding a bit with each step. From the peak, we could see Mount Shasta two-hundred miles to the south and Mount Hood two-hundred miles to the north. The Three Sisters Mountains were also visible to the northwest. We ate lunch on a narrow shelf just below the peak and I had one of the most heart-felt worship experiences of my life! I just said, "Thank you Jesus" over and over again! We serve an Awesome Creator God and from the top of a mountain, His creative power is overwhelmingly. It screams at you!

As I said, it was hot on the mountain that day and we had run out of water by the time we reached the peak. That's when Lee's teacher friend Steve said, "Hey, I have a canister of beer in my backpack"! He had planned to drink that beer to celebrate his climb, but we ended up sharing it to get down the mountain. It's amazing how the carbohydrates in that beer rejuvenated our legs. I have never been more thankful for beer and I can't imagine what our descent would have been like without it.

Lee and I rested our legs for a day and then drove to the Three Sisters Wilderness to climb the Southern Sister. The Three Sisters Wilderness is breathtakingly beautiful! On our ascent of the mountain, we came to a slope that had been cleared of trees by an avalanche, leaving a grassy meadow. This meadow was alive with wild flowers and insects. Lee has a Doctorate degree in Entomology, so he was able to identify almost all of the insects and many of the wildflowers. I still vividly remember him holding an insect between his fingers, pushing up his glasses to get a closer view, and identifying the insect by its technical name. He often stopped to listen to a bird call and quickly identified the species. Spending time with Lee in the wilderness is a pretty amazing experience and I love him like a brother!

Much like the day we climbed Thielsen, it was hot at the peak of the Southern Sister. The mountain is an extinct volcano, with the top blown out, leaving a snow-filled crater. A group of college kids from Boise, ID were making snow angels in the snow, which seemed a great idea on a hot day, so Lee and I joined them. Boy that snow felt good!

Following are the lyrics to a song I wrote about my Brown County roots, which mentions climbing Mount Thielsen with Lee in verse three:

(vs.1) I've been to Colorado and I slept beneath the pines. I scaled the mountains near the Great Divide. I gazed on tundra flowers and I fished the glacial ponds. The photographs are stored here in my mind.

(vs.2) I've walked along the beaches and I heard the ocean roar. I watched the sunset, saw the flash of green. I dived in emerald waters and saw splendor all around. The photographs are stored here in my mind.

(vs.3) I climbed a northwest mountain 'til I almost reached the sky. Lee and I could see two-hundred miles. Shasta was in front of us, Mount Hood was far behind. The photographs are stored here in my mind.

(vs.4) My mom and dad were born here and it's here I trace my line. To pioneers, who cleared and built their farms. Their presence lingers round me as I walk these hills of Brown. I feel like I am held here in their arms.

(chorus) Yes, I've been a lot of places, but I know where I belong. It's here in these forests that I roam. 'Cause home is where the heart is and I know where mine belongs, it's here in my Brown County home.

My Brown County Home by Don Whetstine
2020 UBP ARR

Retirement has allowed me to scratch several things off my bucket list, like climbing mountains with Lee. I am very grateful for this period of my life!

Brown County Sheriff's Department

DISCLAIMER: For the sake of anonymity, I have used very few full names in this book. In the following section, I will refrain from using any names, because the stories deal with sensitive information about persons I met through the Sheriff's Department.

When I retired from New Covenant, I had already spent ten years working as a Jail Chaplain at the Brown County Jail. A year after I retired, our newly elected Sheriff asked me to become a Reserve Deputy and the Department Chaplain. At seventy years of age, I trained to become a Deputy Sheriff. What an honor it was to be sworn in at the completion of my training. It is every little boy's dream to be either a fireman or a policeman and I got to be a Deputy Sheriff at age seventy!

TRAIN, TRAIN, TRAIN

The Sheriff's Department never stops training. The first thing a Police Officer must do is complete a course called Pre-Basic, which is a crash course in Law Enforcement. This was an intensive week of study, approved by the Indiana Law Enforcement Academy, which included both live and video training in the classroom. A Police Officer must understand the Law, which includes The U.S. Constitution, the State Constitution, and any State, County, or City laws and regulations that pertain to your particular jurisdiction and duties as a Police Officer. The rights and jurisdiction of a Police Officer are a vital part of the training. I sweat bullets that week. When I was not in class, I was studying at home. I ate, slept, and breathed Law Enforcement. It had been a long time since I had been in college and, at seventy, this was a challenge. There were daily tests and a humdinger of a final test. I prayed hard that I would pass the final test and I scored 97%. Thank you Jesus!

Tactical Training followed the classroom training. This included take-down, pain and compliance, defense, and handcuffing tactics. I rather enjoyed that part of the training. I got punched, kicked, taken-down, and handcuffed numerous times; but, I got to do the same to others in the class. In one session, I was required to take-down another officer, who stood well above six feet and weighed almost three hundred pounds. Using proper tactics, I was able to throw him down, but he was so broad that I had to borrow an extra set of cuffs to restrain him. I was pretty sore the next day.

We were also required to complete firearms training in the classroom and on the shooting range. I was issued a brand new Sig Sauer P-226 9mm handgun, which was the sweetest pistol I have ever fired. We were required to qualify with a handgun, an assault shotgun, and an AR-15 rifle. We shot for four hours and I did not have to pay for any of the ammunition. Sweet!

We also did monthly training with the Department and a weekend of intensive training each year. I received Pepper Spray, ASP (an extendable baton), and Taser training. I also completed Emergency Vehicle Operation training in the classroom, in a simulator, and on a road course. There is nothing quite like hammering a police cruiser. I was also impressed with how well they stop and corner. I completed STOPS training, which is instruction on how to properly stop a vehicle and approach the occupants. I received Active Shooter training and instruction on how to clear buildings. And, each ysear we were required to qualify with firearms.

Over the fifteen years I served as a Chaplain with the Sheriff's Department, I received excellent training with the Indiana Sheriff's Chaplains Association, which was held at the Hamilton County Sheriff's Department. The training was conducted by many conservative Christian professionals, who served in Law Enforcement, Chaplaincy, and Mental Health. I met some very fine men and women at this training.

Once, when I was returning from Chaplains training in a clearly-marked Sheriff's Department cruiser, I drove around I-465 in Indy at rush hour. My cruise control was set at 55 mph, which was the speed limit, but people usually drive 75 to 80 mph on I-465 during rush hour. I had so many cars bunched-up behind me, I felt like I was driving the pace car at a NASCAR event. No one passed me!

24/7 Service

As the Department Chaplain, I was called out day or night for suicides, accidental deaths, car crashes, and other traumatic events. I made death notifications to families who had lost loved ones. The death notifications to inmates in our jail were especially heart-wrenching. I oversaw Critical Incident Stress Debriefing for officers in the department, who had experienced a traumatic event. And, I served as the Pastor of the Sheriff's Department, ministering to the men and women who served our Department.

I also oversaw ministry to the inmates in our County Jail, which included training the volunteers who were part of our Jail Ministry Team. Most Tuesdays and Thursdays, I was in the jail ministering to the inmates. On Sunday night, I either supervised or led the inmate worship service. One Sunday night, as I sat against the back wall of the chapel with a group of inmates, I began to wonder why I felt so comfortable. It seemed ironic, that I felt more at peace in a worship service with a group of criminals, than I did in a church. I concluded that it was because God had anointed me to be there. There is a peace that comes from being in the place you are supposed to be, doing what God has anointed you to do. Follow the peace and you will find your God-anointed place of service, which may change through the years. Be flexible!

ATTEMPTING TO MINISTER PEACE

One of the first times that I was called out by the department, was to an attempted murder/suicide. A man and his adult daughter were drinking and arguing. The daughter threw a jar of peanut butter at the father, who pulled out his pistol and shot his daughter in the abdomen. He then placed the pistol against his head and shot himself to death. I walked into that chaotic scene at 2:30 AM and tried to bring peace to the distraught wife and mother. It is pretty incredible what Law Enforcement deals with while most people sleep peacefully.

On a beautiful spring morning, I got a call from our Chief Deputy, who summoned me to a home where a teenage girl had committed suicide. As I hung up the phone, my heart sank. I knew this girl! I jumped into uniform and hurried to the address. The scene was surreal! It was a beautiful spring morning, with trees budding and birds singing; but, as I pulled up to the house, I could see this beautiful young lady hanging by her neck on the back porch. The coroner had just arrived and several of our deputies were at the scene. I gathered the family members in the front yard, while the Chief Deputy and the Coroner completed a death investigation. I consoled the family as best I could and tried to speak comforting words to them, but I felt very inadequate. I was attempting to bring peace where there was little peace to be found. I don't think I will ever forget that scene. I often drive past that area and grieve that this beautiful young lady did not find the help she needed to go on living.

I experienced many such scenes through my years as a Chaplain. It is only by the grace of God that I had anything to bring to those situations.

Jail House Religion

I have often heard the spiritual renewal that takes place in jail called, "jail house religion", which is an inference that it is not real. I beg to differ! I had fifteen years as a Chaplain, to watch God transform inmate's lives. While incarcerated, many inmates do very well, because they have changed their nouns—persons, places, and things. They thrive in that controlled environment. It is when they are released from jail that the real test begins. If the inmate is a "frequent flyer" (often in jail), they have probably worn-out their family, if they ever had a loving, supporting family. At one time, we estimated that up to 90% of the persons incarcerated at our jail were addicted to Meth, Heroin, or both. That is the major demon that makes lasting renewal difficult for a former inmate. When they are released from jail, it is often their old druggy buddies waiting to pick them up and supply them with whatever they need, or don't need. A released inmate is often homeless, has multiple felonies on their record, and has a suspended driver's license. How do you tell that person to get a good job and improve themselves?

INMATE MINISTRY ROUTINE

Tuesdays and Thursdays often found me in the jail ministering to the inmates. My routine was to go back to the big board in the hallway near the booking desk, where the names of all the inmates are listed. Checking for recently incarcerated inmates, I often recognized the names, because they were frequent flyers. I made a list of the inmates I planned to see and asked the guards to call them out one-by-one to the interview room. I invited newcomers to our Sunday night worship service, gave them a Celebrate Recovery Bible, and talked and prayed with them. About 50% of my time spent with inmates involved addictions counseling. Though I am not a licensed addiction counselor, my Chaplain's training and years of helping addicted people were my qualifications. I helped the inmates work through the eight principles in the Celebrate Recovery Bible, which is a shortened version of the twelve steps of Alcoholics Anonymous and encouraged them to attend recovery groups that met in our jail. In addition, I helped them find treatment programs and recovery meetings, once released from jail. Through the years, we lost several former inmates to drug overdoses. They were my friends! It was gut-wrenching to pour my heart into someone, who ended up dead under a bridge with a needle in their arm. In my fifteen years with the Department, it never got easier.

I often went back to the Drunk Tank, asked the guard to roll the door, and talked to the inmates who had been recently arrested. Some of them, high on Meth, had not slept for days. After they came down from their high, they would sleep for a day or two before beginning withdrawal, referred to as "itching and twitching", which is exactly what they experienced. It was hard to watch.

Occasionally, I conducted a Bible study in a cell block. A cell block has an open gathering area with eight cells on two levels. A cell block could hold up to sixteen inmates, but our jail was never that crowded. I loved to minister in the cell blocks, because I met inmates who did not attend our worship service. Once when I was conducting a Bible study in a cell block, an inmate rushed out of his cell, swearing at me and wanting to fight. He hated Jews and had reacted to my last name. As he stood in my face, swearing at me, I found it laughable and that's what I did. I laughed hysterically! He was so flabbergasted that he stormed back into his cell and locked himself in. Looking back, I think that was a God-thing, a perfect way to defuse the situation. In fifteen years of ministry in the jail, that was the only time that I was ever threatened by an inmate. I never felt afraid or intimidated while ministering in the jail. I always knew that God had my back.

I said earlier, up to 90% of the inmates incarcerated at our jail are addicted to Meth, Heroin, or both. Today, almost all Heroin is laced with Fentanyl, which is the drug that is killing our young people. Fentanyl is so dangerous that Deputies were trained to wear latex gloves when frisking someone. If you stick your bare hand into someone's pocket and make contact with Fentanyl, you could end up in the ER. An overdose can be neutralized with Naloxone, which has saved many lives. Some Heroin addicts actually carry Naloxone in their pocket, but once you go unconscious, you cannot administer it yourself. It's lights out!

One morning, the Department summoned me to the home of a former inmate who had overdosed overnight, with Naloxone close to the bed where he died. He had planned to enter a treatment facility later that day. That was a very sad day for the family and for me, because I knew them all very well. On another occasion, a teen from our county died of an overdose and, when the Coroner arrived at the scene, the teen still had the tourniquet around his arm and the syringe stuck in his arm. The teen thought that he was injecting Heroin, but the toxicology report indicated he had injected almost pure Fentanyl. The Coroner said the teen was probably dead before he hit the floor. That is tragic!

My one-on-one ministry to inmates was to men only. Occasionally, I did a death notification with a female inmate or ministered to a female inmate under special circumstances. In such cases, I always had a Corrections Officer present, preferably a female officer. Our jail policy is that men minister to men and women minister to women. It is a good policy. A couple of women on our ministry team ministered to the female inmates.

Some incredible ministry took place during my Tuesday and Thursday meetings with the inmates. In the course of the conversation, when I asked an inmate about his father, he often pulled up his shirt to wipe his tears. The inmates in our jails and prisons have bad relationships with their fathers, if they have a relationship at all. As a result, they have deep father wounds. I was a father figure to the inmates and did my best to show them what a good father looks like.

RACIST BIKER

One Sunday night, an inmate came to our worship service, sat with his arms crossed, and a glare on his face. I greeted him at the end of the service and talked with him a bit. He had heard that I was a biker and told me that he was also. As he left the service, I noticed he had a swastika tattooed on the back of his neck. Each week he returned and his countenance never changed. It was a bit intimidating to see this burly man glaring at me while I attempted to lead worship or preach. Sometimes, inmates attended the worship service as an excuse to get out of their cell block, so I figured that this was his case.

One night he attended our worship with an altogether different attitude. He told me that he did some serious thinking after he went back to his cell the previous Sunday. He said he began to cry like a baby and spent the night repenting of his sins and asking God to forgive him. After we baptized him, he began to grow quickly in his new found faith. A couple of teenage boys were arrested and, because of the serious nature of their crime, were charged as adults and housed with the adult population in our jail. This inmate warned the other inmates that "if they messed with those boys, they would be messing with him"! No one messed with the boys.

When my friend missed the worship service one Sunday, the other inmates said that he had been locked down for tattooing, which was against the rules. The inmates charred toilet paper in a microwave, mixed the ashes with Vaseline to create ink, dipped a sharp object wrapped with thread in the ink, and tattooed one another. When the inmate returned to the worship service, I noticed that the swastika on the back of his neck had been covered with a cross. He began to minister effectively to the inmates, so we designated him our "Inside Chaplain" and met with him weekly to discuss his ministry and pray for him.

ROLE MODEL

A young man was booked at our jail and came to the inmate worship service the next Sunday night. I knew him, for I had known his family for years. He was addicted to Meth, which had caused his life to spiral out of control. As I greeted him and talked with him at the service, he immediately began to wipe tears. He had a tender heart, regardless of where his addiction had taken him. Because of the seriousness of his crimes, I expected the court to remand him to DOC to spend time in prison, but he was allowed to serve his sentence at our jail. I spent a lot of time with this brother, who became a model prisoner. The Jail Commander soon made him a Trustee and allowed him to work in the kitchen at the jail.

A couple of years before, the Sheriff told me we needed a role model, someone who had gotten free from Meth and could help others to do the same. When this inmate was about to be released from jail, I reminded the Sheriff of that conversation and suggested that this young man could be the role model we were looking for. I asked if I could make him part of our Jail Ministry Team. Usually, persons with felonies on their record are not allowed to serve on the ministry team. The Sheriff thought for a moment and said, "Keep him on a short leash". I promised that he would only come in the jail with me. All the people who served on our Jail Ministry Team had to complete a criminal background check. I asked the Sheriff if this man needed a background check and he said, "Oh, I think we know his background".

That was the start of a great partnership in ministry with this young man. I soon gave him opportunities to speak in our worship service. The guys listened attentively, because many of them had taken drugs and committed crimes with him. He had a major impact on the inmates and the Sheriff soon allowed me to take him back in the cell blocks to help minister to the inmates. Although, being in the cell blocks triggered a lot of bad memories. Once, when we were in the cell blocks, I thought he was going to have a panic attack. When I used my fob to open the door out of the secure area of the jail, he bolted through the door. I praise God for this brother, who continues to live clean and sober. He has helped many people in our county who are struggling with addiction.

THE ARYAN

A group of men associated with the Aryan Brotherhood were arrested in our county after they held a family captive and stole their possessions. The Aryan Brotherhood is a racist prison gang. Their counterpart on the street is the Skinheads. One of the men arrested, a past president of the Brotherhood, was big, angry, and mean. Locking him up was like putting a Coyote in a cage—he became unhinged. One day, when he went berserk in his cell block, the guards had the unwanted responsibility of restraining him and locking him in his cell. With backup from the Road Deputies, a sizable group of officers went back to the cell block to restrain the man. However, before the officers reached the cell block, another inmate held up his Bible and began to pray over the Aryan, who calmed down and began to cry. By the time the officers reached the cell block, the Aryan was totally compliant and allowed the officers to lock him in his cell.

The following Sunday, he came to the worship service, walked up to me, and said, "You've got to explain something to me"! Then he told me what he had experienced in the cell block that week and ended by asking, "Was that God or something"? I said, "Yes, that was God and He was saying hello to you". P.J., a member of our ministry team, and I began to meet regularly with him for Bible study and prayer. Eventually, he accepted Christ as his Savior and we baptized him. We did baptisms in a stock tank that we dragged into the Sally Port, which is a secure entry for patrol cars bringing prisoners to the jail. In the past, we had transported inmates to the Christian Church for baptism, but their hands and feet had to be shackled and additional officers were needed for security. Back in that day, Sheriff Buck Stogsdill usually read from the sixth chapter of Romans before the baptisms. Buck passed away midway through my time at the Sheriff's Department and I really miss the brother. Buck was a great guy!

The former Aryan just barely fit into the stock tank and, as P.J. and I lowered him in the water, a lot of the water splashed out. He began to grow quickly in his walk with Christ. One day, when we met with him, he said he wanted to become a preacher. Then, he pulled up his shirt to expose his Aryan Brotherhood tattoos and said, "How can I preach with this stuff on my body"? He also had the numbers 88 and a swastika tattooed on him. The eighth letter of the alphabet is H, so 88 represents HH, or Heil Hitler. I responded, "Brother, those tattoos will preach, just tell your story".

At his trial, he stood before the court and denounced the Aryan Brotherhood, which he said "had destroyed his life". He then confessed his faith in Jesus Christ and announced that he was going to live for Him. He was sentenced to three years in prison. After publically denouncing The Brotherhood, I feared they would kill him in prison. When he got to prison, he found another former Aryan, who had become a Christian, and the two of them became Chaplain's Assistants. He said the Aryans seemed to be afraid of them and avoided them.

IS THAT LIKE BEING SAVED?

A very young inmate came to our service one Sunday night. He was very friendly and polite. I wondered why such a nice kid was in jail. I often felt that way about some of the inmates. I knew exactly why others were in jail. I had a nice chat with him before he went back to his cell block. The next Sunday, he was in our service again and asked to talk with me after the service. He told me he had not been in church very much, but had gone back to his cell the previous week, thought about the things that he had heard, and wept as he told God every bad thing that he could remember. Then he asked God to forgive him of his sins and asked Jesus to come into his heart and change him. He asked me, "Is that kind of like being saved"? I told him that was exactly like being saved. I prayed with him and we soon baptized him.

Big Guy

A man was arrested for possession of the largest amount of Meth ever seized in our county. When he came to the worship service the next Sunday, I chatted with him before and after the service. He was a big tough-looking guy in his mid fifties, with long white hair and beard. I asked if I could meet with him during the coming week and he consented. Later in the week, I met with the inmate and learned a bit about his history. He said he had used Heroin until he could no longer get high, so he switched to Meth and used that until he could no longer get high. He said he was drinking a quart of vodka a day at the time of his arrest and that did not give him a buzz. Addiction is partly defined as an "allergic like condition", which means that your body reacts to drugs and alcohol in a similar manner as to an allergen. After a while, your body develops resistance to this supposed allergen and you no longer get high, but the drugs may have already done serious damage to your body. This man was a prime example of that. Even though he no longer got high from drugs and alcohol, he was suffering from a host of medical issues. I gave him a Bible and we began meeting weekly for Bible study and prayer. I really liked this guy and we quickly became friends.

The Jail Commander called me one morning and asked me to make a death notification with this inmate, whose mother had died unexpectedly. When I summoned him to the interview room, he entered with a big smile. That smile was soon replaced with a look of extreme sadness as I told him of his mother's passing. This big tough guy turned into a basket case and wept as hard as I have ever seen anyone weep. He loved his mother!

As I continued to meet with him, he became like a brother to me. He had been charged with drug distribution, but argued that he was not distributing drugs when arrested, just in possession of them. He believed that his lawyer could plead that charge down to a lesser offence, but because of the amount of Meth in his possession, the court charged him with intent to distribute and sentenced him to fifteen years in prison. Considering his age and physical condition, I am pretty sure he will die in prison. I was at the jail the morning the U.S. Marshalls came to transport him to prison. One of the Marshalls gave him a great Jesus talk as he put the shackles on his hands and feet. I encouraged the inmate, prayed for him, and told him that I loved him. Then, I watched him shuffle down the hallway to the Sally Port in the custody of the Marshalls. He stopped midway, turned around, and said, "I love you man"! My eyes began to leak.

CAGE FIGHTER

A young man, booked at our jail for battery, attended our worship service and I liked him immediately. He constantly wore a big grin and was very comical. One day, I met with him in the interview room and got to know more about him. He told me he had spent most of his teenage years in jail. He had a horrid childhood at the hands of a physically abusive father, who constantly beat him. One day I noticed scars on the back of his head and asked where he got them. He said he got the scars from his dad. He suffered from PTSD and Explosive Anger Disorder from his upbringing. He had been a cage fighter, so when people pushed his buttons, they tended to get hurt. He told me that when he became really angry, he sort of blacked-out and didn't remember what happened. The inmates in his cell block began pushing his buttons, so fights occurred. He was locked-down repeatedly for fighting and finally got a forty-five day lockdown in a holding cell. Usually, when an inmate is locked-down, he is locked in his cell. For serious incidents, an inmate is sent to a holding cell in the hallway near the booking desk. The holding cells are what inmates in prison refer to as "the hole". A holding cell is small, has a thick steel door with one small window and a bean hole, which is a flap in the door large enough for a food tray. The bunk, made of solid steel, is bolted to the concrete floor. It has a three inch mattress and the inmate is issued a thick wool blanket, but no pillow. There is a stainless steel toilet with no seat and a stainless steel sink. The lights in a holding cell remain on 24/7 and cameras monitor the inmate constantly. It's not a nice place. While detained in a holding cell, an inmate is not allowed visitors. The only one allowed to visit them, is the Department Chaplain, which was me.

A couple of times a week, I asked the guards to roll the electronic door to his holding cell and I went in to sit and talk with him. I gave him a Bible, which he began to study. Before long, he had lots of questions for me about the Bible. I eventually prayed with him to receive Jesus as his Savior and baptized him when he was released from the holding cell. He had some severe episodes with anxiety, which sometimes resulted in panic attacks. I taught him about Grounding Techniques and pointed him to several Psalms, which he found helpful in relieving his anxiety. I came in to see him one day and noticed that he had a towel folded on the floor next to his bunk. He said that he knelt on the towel when he prayed for several hours straight. Wow!

One day I came in to talk with him and found him talking through his bean hole to a lady in a holding cell across the hallway, who was listening through her bean hole. He was encouraging her to trust Christ and was praying for her. That was so way cool! I decided to not interrupt and visited other inmates.

Once released from the holding cell, he became a model prisoner. I appointed him Chaplain's Assistant and he helped me prepare the chapel for our worship services. He asked me to start a Bible study in his cell block and most of the inmates in the cell block attended. He occasionally asked to speak at our worship service and I was really impressed with his ability to communicate with the inmates.

After his trial, he was sent to prison for three years. He became a Chaplin's Assistant in prison and shared his faith with many of the inmates. Today, he is out of prison, off parole, and owns a painting company. He gained custody of his daughter and, at the time I write this, is engaged to be married. He is also back in the cage as an MMA fighter. His Face Book site declares that he is "First and Foremost a man of God".

DEPUTY DON

I really enjoyed being a Reserve Deputy. I patrolled with the other officers and got involved in whatever they were doing. I actually liked responding to domestic disturbances, because it was an opportunity to separate couples and counsel them, much like I did as a Pastor. Working traffic details was also enjoyable. I helped chase bad guys, serve warrants, make traffic stops, and take people to jail. Once they were in jail, I switched to my Chaplain role.

One day, I accompanied a group of officers to serve a warrant that seemed routine, until dispatch called to inform us that the person's Face Book page had a picture of him with an AR-15. Then things got tense, because an AR-15 round will penetrate a protective vest. I helped respond to several suicide attempts and overdoses. I was also at the scene of several serious car and motorcycle crashes. One of the last times I was called out by the Department, was to a motorcycle crash involving a couple in their mid-fifties. The lady lay dead on the highway, with a huge pool of blood under her head and her eyes wide open. Her husband was entangled in a guard rail. I told our Chief Deputy that I would probably quit riding my Harley after that. I sold it shortly thereafter.

One of my favorite assignments was to assist the Resource Officers at our county schools. Sprunica Elementary was my favorite, because my granddaughter was a student there and I loved interacting with her and her cute friends. A couple of our elementary schools are located in remote areas of the county and the staff and teachers appreciated our presence in their schools. I always parked the patrol car where it was easily visible to anyone who may want to do harm to our students.

More than anything, I loved the camaraderie with the other officers in the Department. I had some very special conversations with them as we patrolled together. Wearing the uniform of the Sheriff's Department was one of the greatest honors of my lifetime. I loved representing the Department and protecting our community.

Retiring as Chaplain and Reserve Deputy

In 2018, I was dealing with some health problems that had sucked my energy. The doctors had started me on four new medications that were kicking my butt. I was tired and I needed to rest and get healthy again. I was also suffering from compassion fatigue. I had heard about that for years and can now testify that it is real. I met with the Sheriff and told him I needed to resign as a Chaplain and Reserve Deputy. He said, "I refuse your resignation. We are going to retire you". In 2018, the Department retired me as a Chaplain and a Reserve Deputy at age seventy-five.

NEW UNIFORM WITH SAME DEPARTMENT

As I got healthier, I began assisting Jenny Sue with monthly food deliveries with TRIAD. TRIAD stands for; The Right Information And Direction. TRIAD members wear Sheriff's Department uniforms and drive department vehicles, but do not carry guns or have arrest powers. I completed training and was sworn in as a TRIAD volunteer. TRIAD visits vulnerable people in Brown County to check on their well being, some of whom live alone in rather remote areas. A lot of what TRIAD does is social in nature. We visited with people and inquired about their needs. Jenny Sue and I served as a team. I did not serve very long with TRIAD, but I really appreciate the people with whom Jenny Sue and I served and the service we performed. TRIAD is wonderful organization and an important arm of our Sheriff's Department.

New Priorities

At the close of 2022, I was contemplating turning eighty and feeling the need to reevaluate my priorities for the twilight years of my life. I knew that it was time to let my service at the Sheriff's Department go. I wanted to focus on the things that were closest to the heart of this old dog. Jenny Sue soon came to the same conclusion about the Sheriff's Department and we both tendered our resignations from TRIAD. At the conclusion of our last official duty, it was sad to call dispatch and report that Brown County 8-10 and Brown County 8-15 were 10-42. Jenny Sue had served with TRIAD for five years. I had served eighteen years as Jail Chaplain, Department Chaplain, Reserve Deputy, and TRIAD volunteer. My only regret with the Sheriff's Department is that I did not start sooner, so that I could have served longer. It was such an honor to serve those eighteen years with the fine people who are the Brown County Sheriff's Department. Members of the Marine Corp declare that they are Marines forever. I feel the same about the Sheriff's Department. I took three oaths with the Department as a Jail Chaplain, Reserve Deputy, and TRIAD. I will always honor those oaths.

Our new list of priorities are; God, family, our own soul-care, Silver Sneakers, and writing/playing/singing our music.

SILVER SNEAKERS

We love our Silver Sneakers group that meets at the Brown County YMCA. Jenny Sue has led this exercise class for twelve years and I am her Emergency Assistant. "Emergency" may mean that I can start your heart or stop your bleeding, since I have had CPR, AED, and First Aid training. I also help lead the class in the absence of Jenny Sue's other assistants. One of the Silver Sneakers said the fellowship with the Sneakers is a lot like a church group. I concur and Jenny Sue and I feel very blessed to be shepherding our flock of Silver Sneakers.

MUSIC

J enny Sue and I began singing together in college and I have played guitar and written music for years. A few years back, I taught Jenny Sue to play bass guitar and we now play together when we sing. A friend of our family built Jenny Sue's custom bass guitar. It is one fine instrument and it looks, sounds, and plays great. We often play and sing at our church or other places we are invited. Our daughter Sharianne is also a singer, song writer, and guitar player. When she performs, Jenny Sue and I sometimes give her a break in the middle of her set, by performing some of our music. It's been fun!

I long dreamed of playing on the streets of Nashville, Indiana as a witness to the many tourists who fill our town. I was inspired by my friends John Franz and Mister Bojangels, who were consummate Street Musicians before they passed. I began singing on the street last fall and Jenny Sue soon joined me. She was reluctant at first, but once she tried it, she was hooked. We can now proudly say that we are Street Musicians, or Street Buskers, and we love it. We claimed a spot on the Village Green in the middle of Nashville and, on a nice day, we play and sing for several hours. One day a young girl danced on the sidewalk in front of us as we played. That was special! On another day, three ladies stopped to listen, turned the sidewalk into a dance floor, and country line danced as we played my song "Bean Blossom Redneck". As long as we repeated the song, they kept on dancing. Wow, that was fun! We met a lot of nice people and shared our faith with many of them. As I write, it's winter and we are looking forward to spring to get back on the street.

CONCLUSION

Certain sections of this book were a bit intimidating to write and I felt like I was standing naked in public. I have revealed intimate details about how God has spoken to me and led me through the years. I am apprehensive that some will think I am some kind of religious weirdo, but I am just someone who has sought to discern God's voice. As you have read in the book, much of my ministry was conducted about a yard from the gates of hell, with extremely broken people. I needed supernatural guidance and power to do my ministry. I do not expect God to work in your life in the same manner as in mine. I do encourage you to seek to discern how God speaks to you and leads you. People are quick to say that the primary way that God speaks to us is through the Bible. I totally agree, but I found that the Bible did not give detailed directions for all the difficult situations I encountered in ministry. That is why God put His Spirit in us, to guide us in the areas where the Bible does not fill in the blanks.

I never trust an experience that I cannot support from the Bible. Some allege that the revelatory gifts of the Spirit ceased at the end of the Apostolic Age, or that God no longer speaks to men at all. I am just saying, this has not been my experience! Years ago, I was listening to a Bible College Professor speak at a convention. He said, "We need to get away from all this subjective stuff and contain ourselves in the objectivity of God's Word". Although the statement sounded very scholarly, I wondered if the man had ever considered that the Bible IS a history account of men's subjective experiences with God. If men did not have subjective experiences with God, we would not have the Bible! That's my story and I'm sticking to it. You can argue with my theology, but you can't argue with my story, for I am the one who lived it! I am getting close to grinding a theological axe, so I will move on.

I am also apprehensive that some will think I consider myself spiritually superior, because of the way God has spoken to me and led me. Let me assure you, this is not the case! I deal with the same temptations that you do. At my most vulnerable times, I have been very close to becoming a spiritual train wreck! I have watched men and women, who seemed more spiritual than I, fall into grievous sin. It is only by the grace of God that I am still standing.

Some people might think I am really smart to have made the choices I have made in my ministry. Actually, I have been rather clueless most of my life. I just listened to the still small voice of God in my spirit and followed His direction. Jesus didn't call His followers "knowers", He called them "believers". I am simply a believer, a follower, a Jesus Freak!

Well, there's my story, as best I remember it. I praise God that I have lived a pretty incredible story. I wept and praised Him numerous times as I recalled the wonderful memories included in this book. God has been so good to me!

As I said in the introduction, I hope my story encourages you to live your own big story. We serve an awesome God, Who can surely enable that. May God bless you.

ACKNOWLEDGMENTS

I could not have authored this book without the help of my wife Jenny Sue. She helped me remember past events and phrase some of the sentences in the book. She also researched word usage and offered many suggestions on what to include and not to include in the book.

Editorial services were performed by Two Sisters—Jenny and Jessy.

The only copyrighted materials quoted in this book are Scriptures from The Holy Bible, New International Version©, NIV©, Copyright © 1973, 1978, 1984, 2011 by Biblia, Inc.©, published by Zondervan.

I am indebted to friends and family members who encouraged and supported me in the completion of the manuscript.

Most of all, I am indebted to God The Father, The Lord Jesus Christ, and The Holy Spirit who anointed and inspired me to live the wonderful life of service to the Kingdom of God chronicled in this book.

CPSIA information can be obtained
at www.ICGtesting.com
Printed in the USA
JSHW011237250623
43707JS00001B/3